DEAR ITALY..a painted story

debbi saccomanno chan

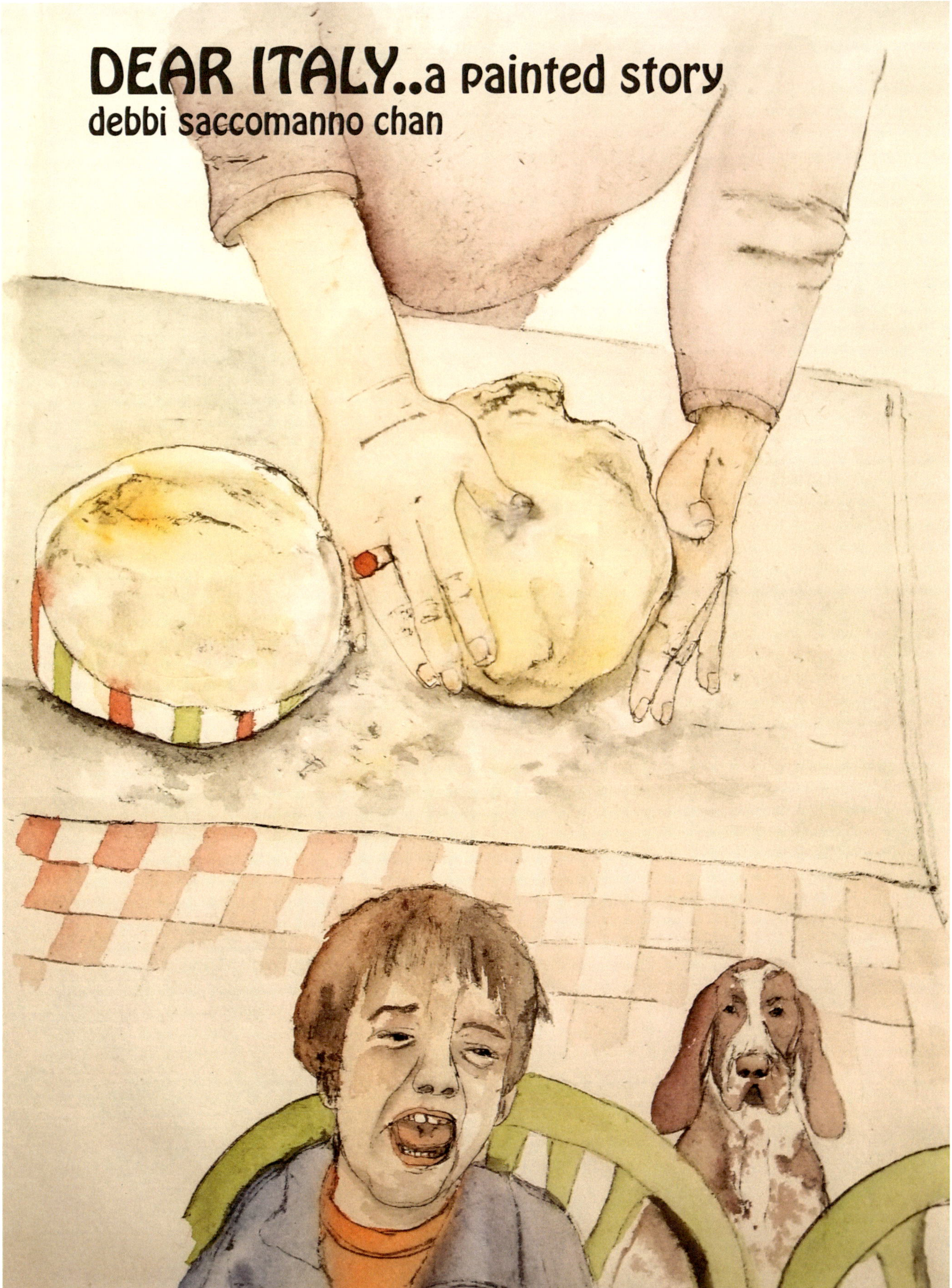

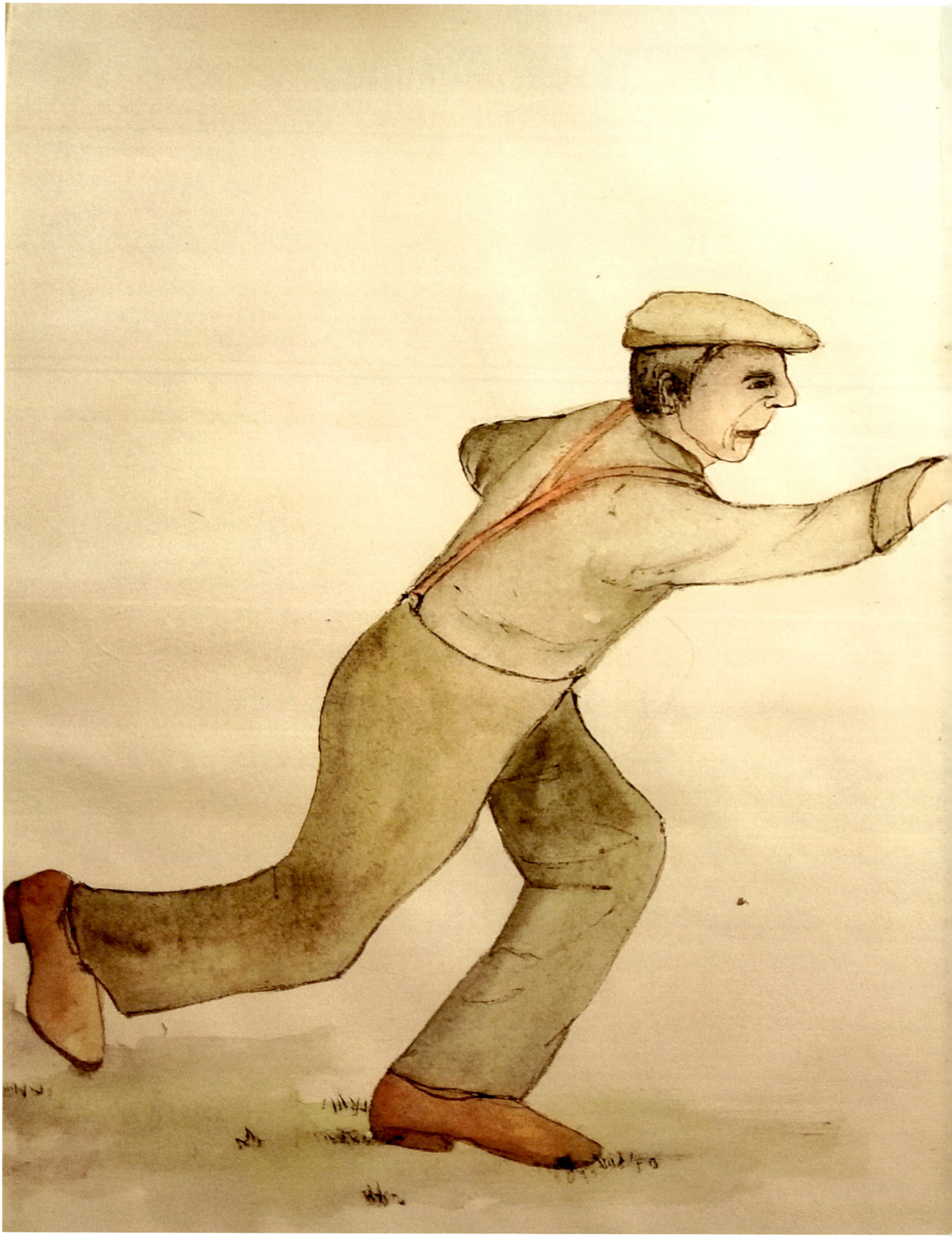

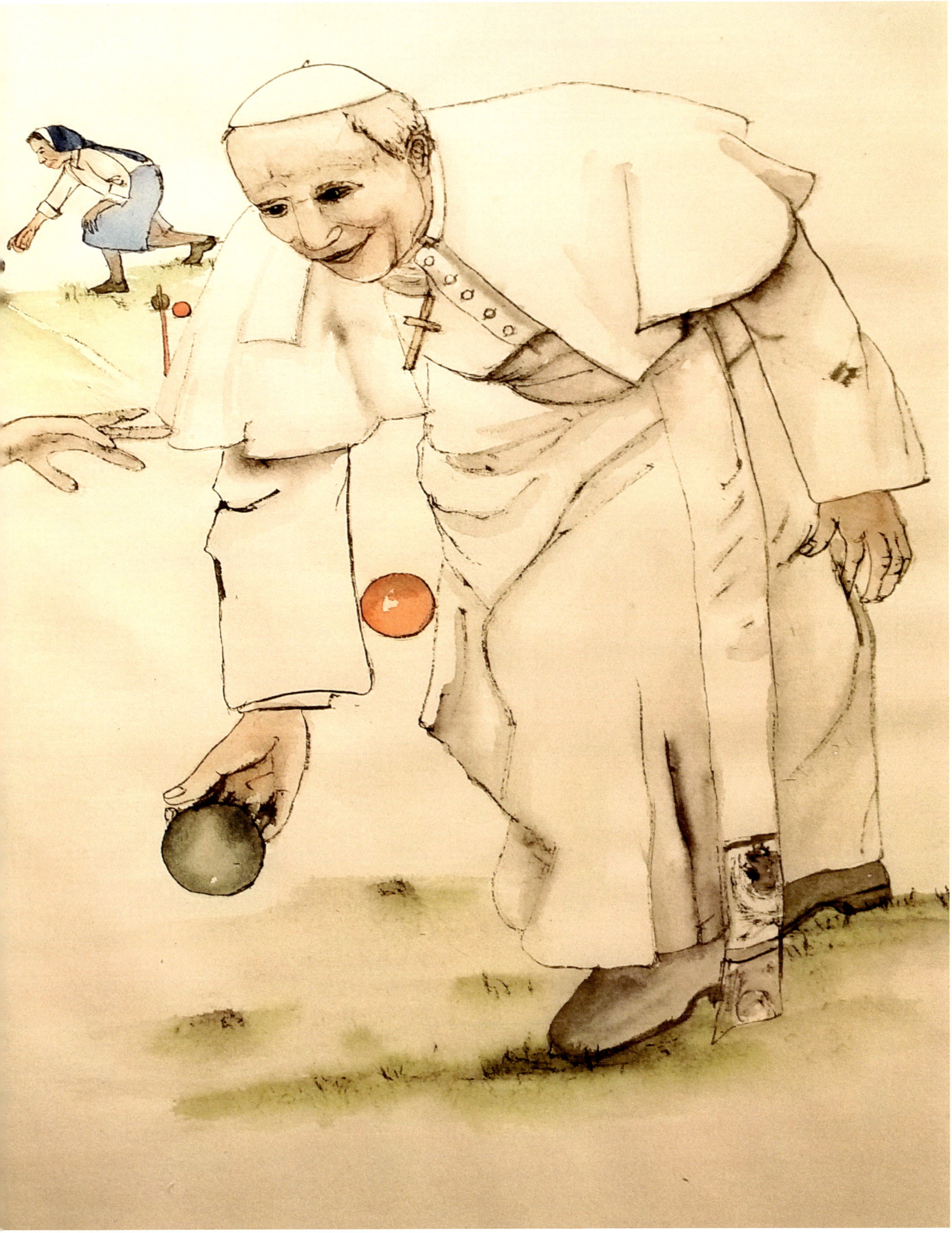

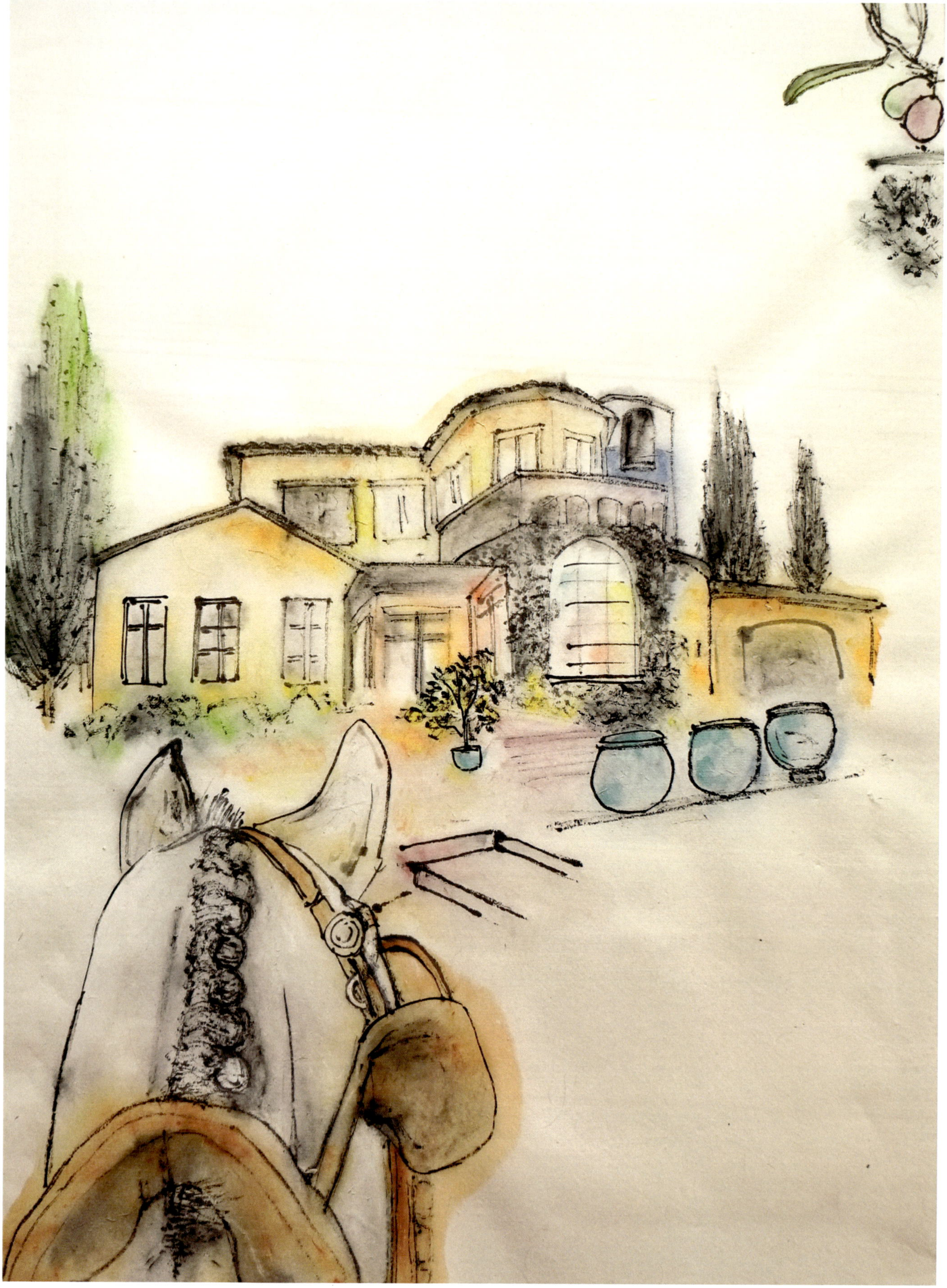

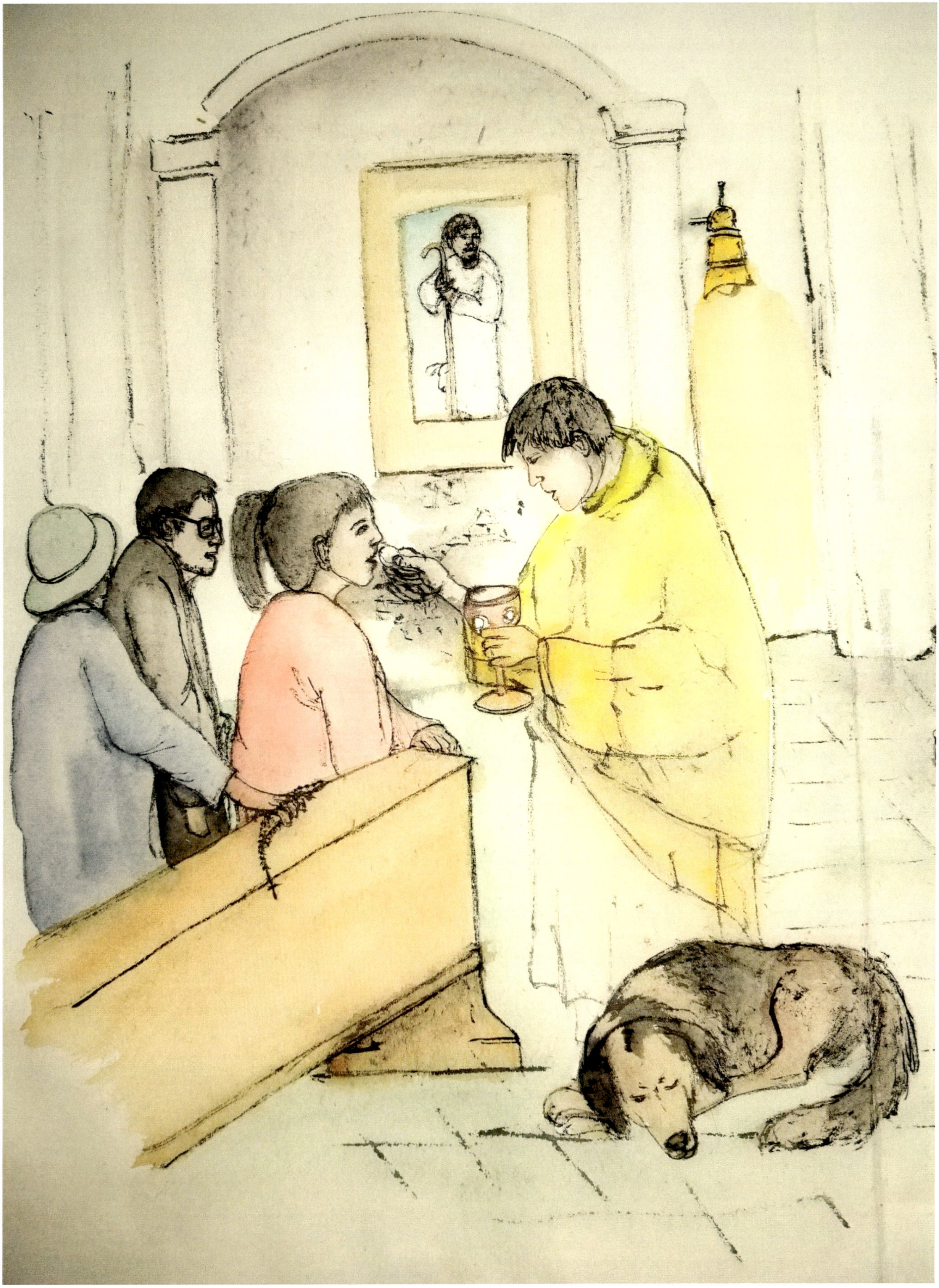

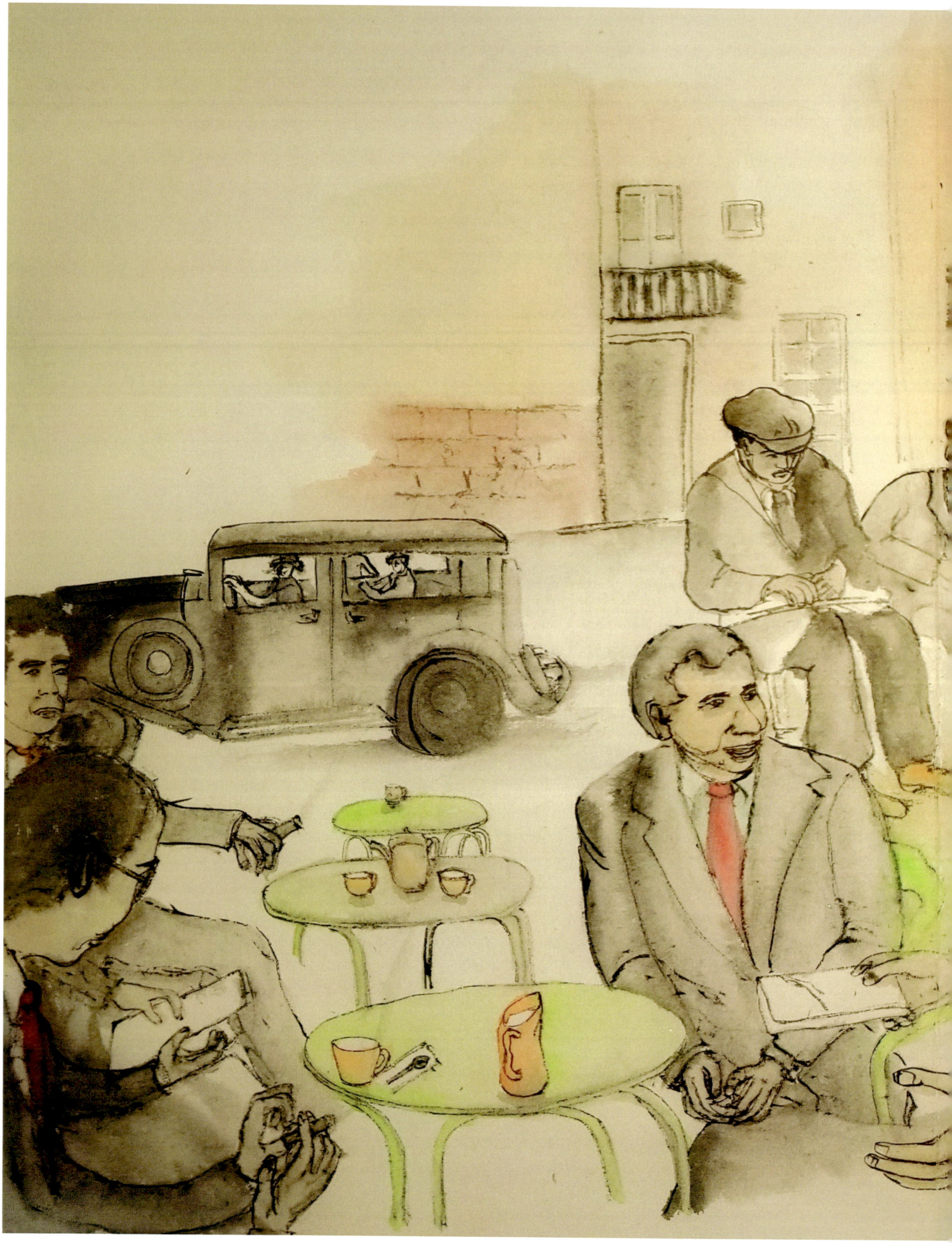

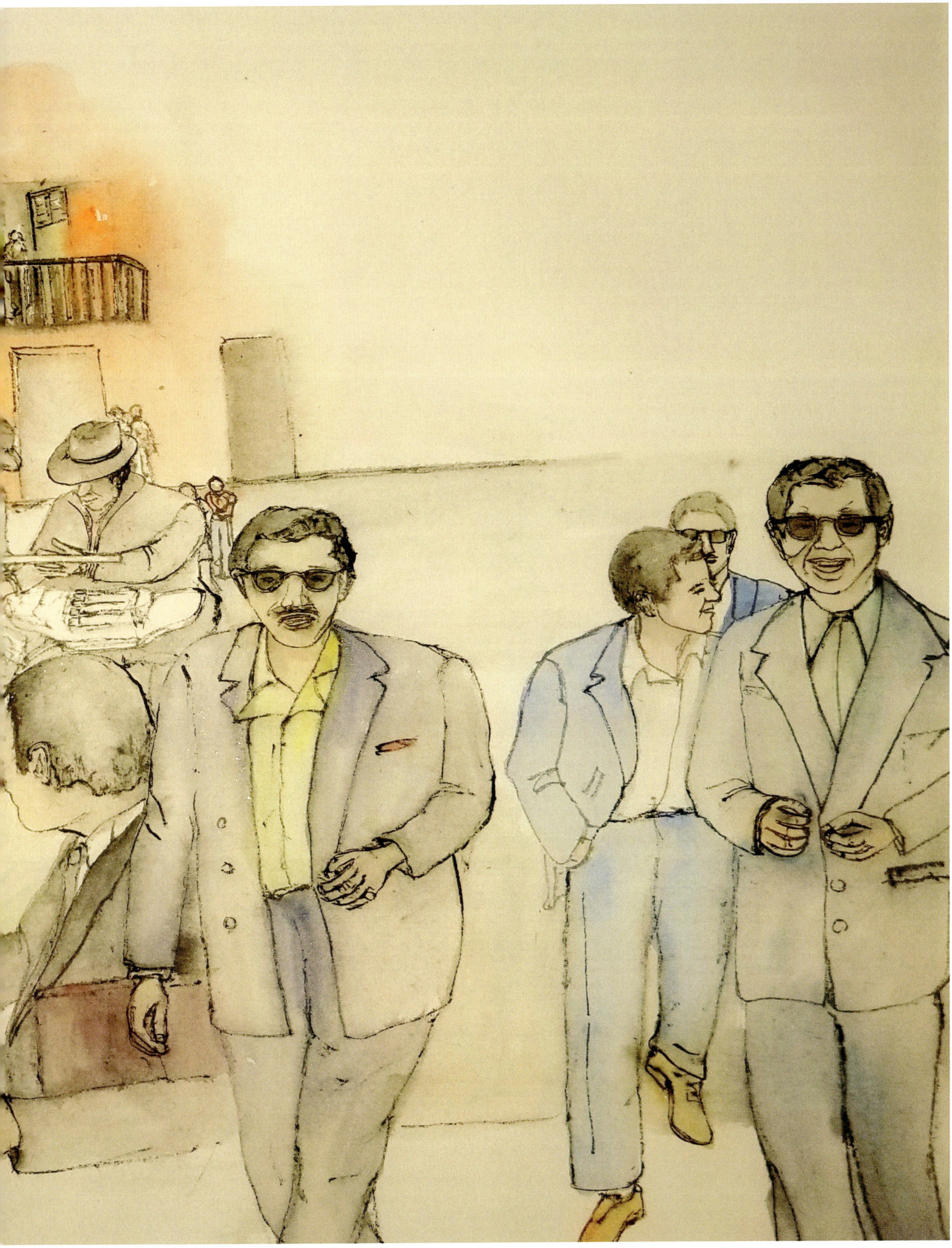

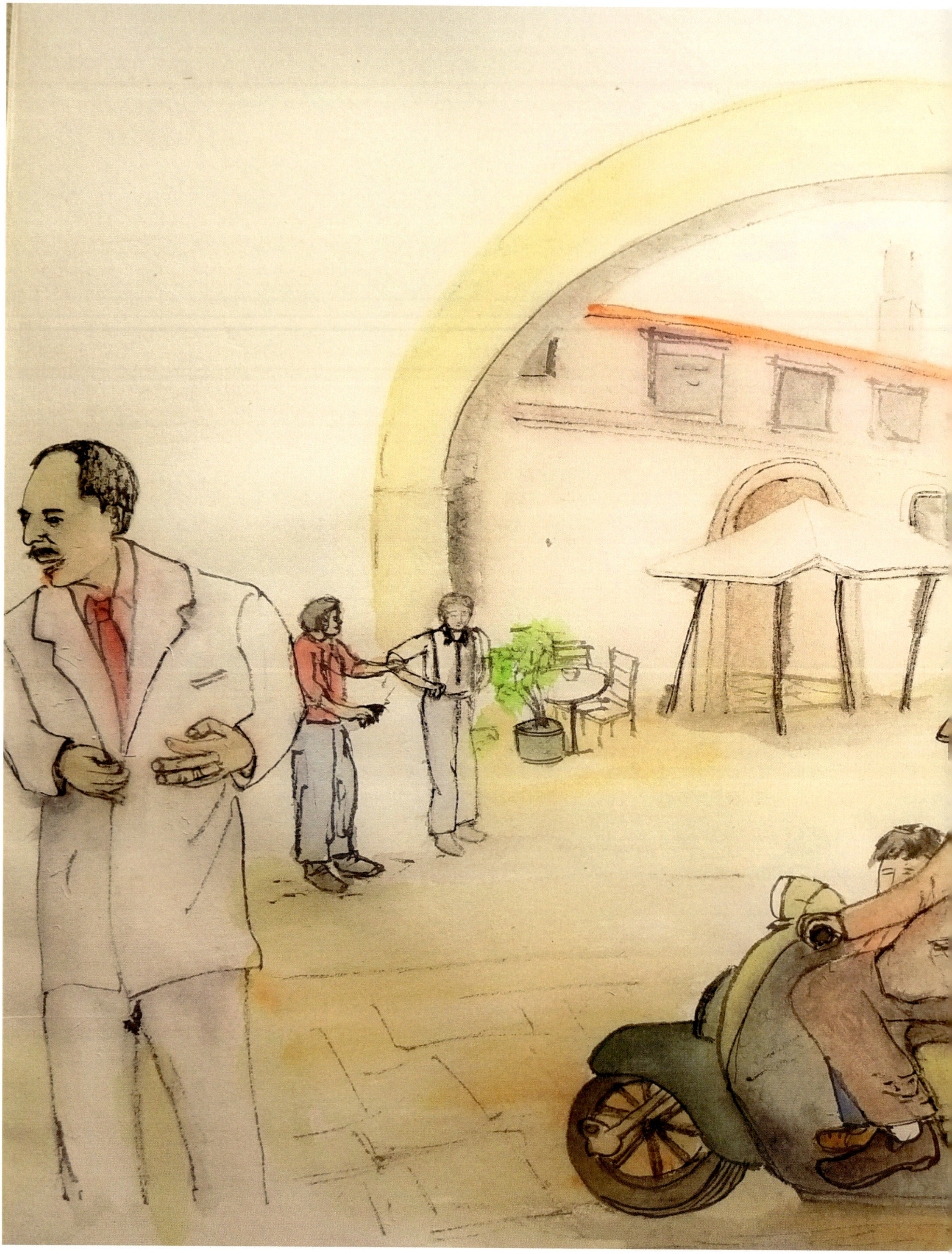

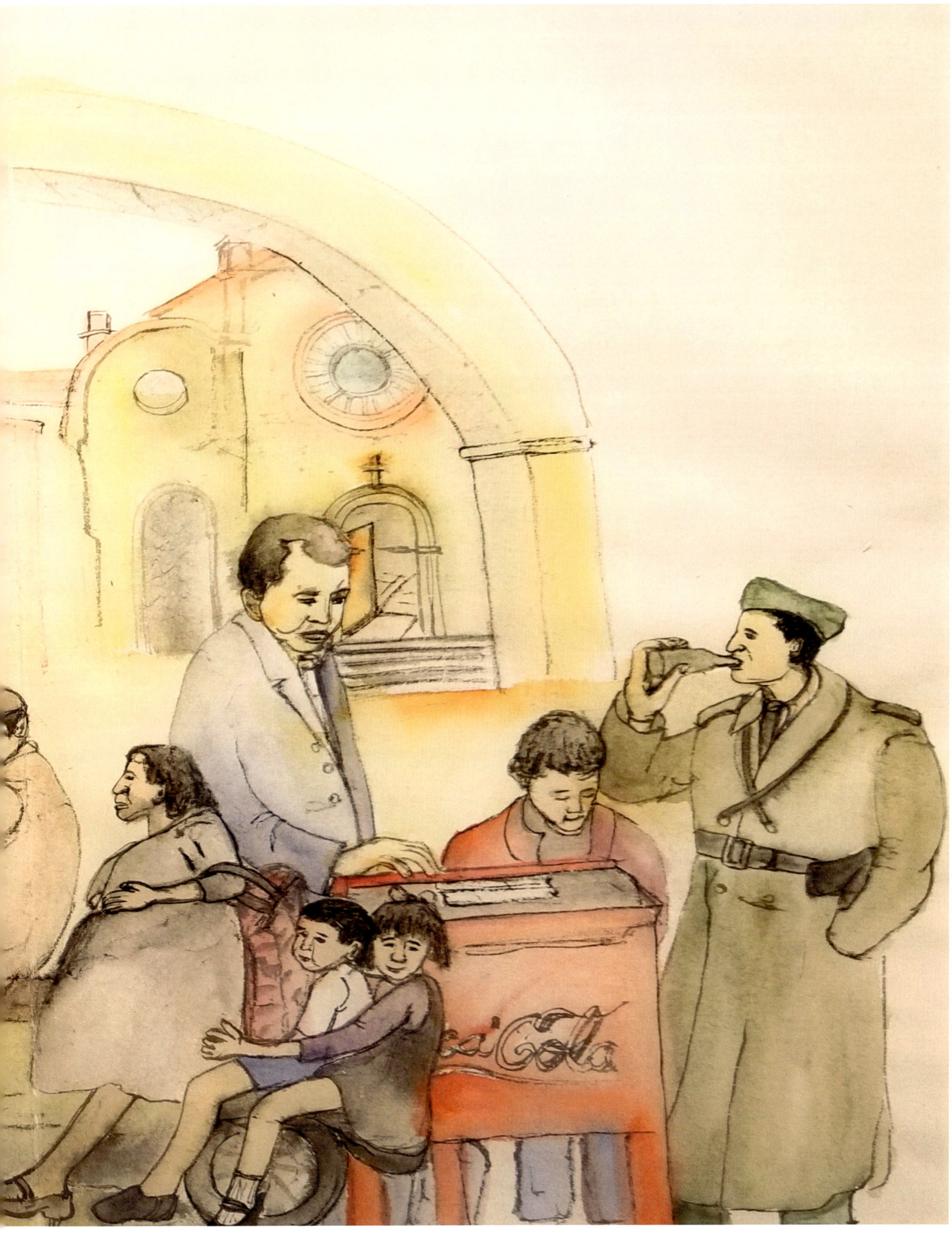
Cola

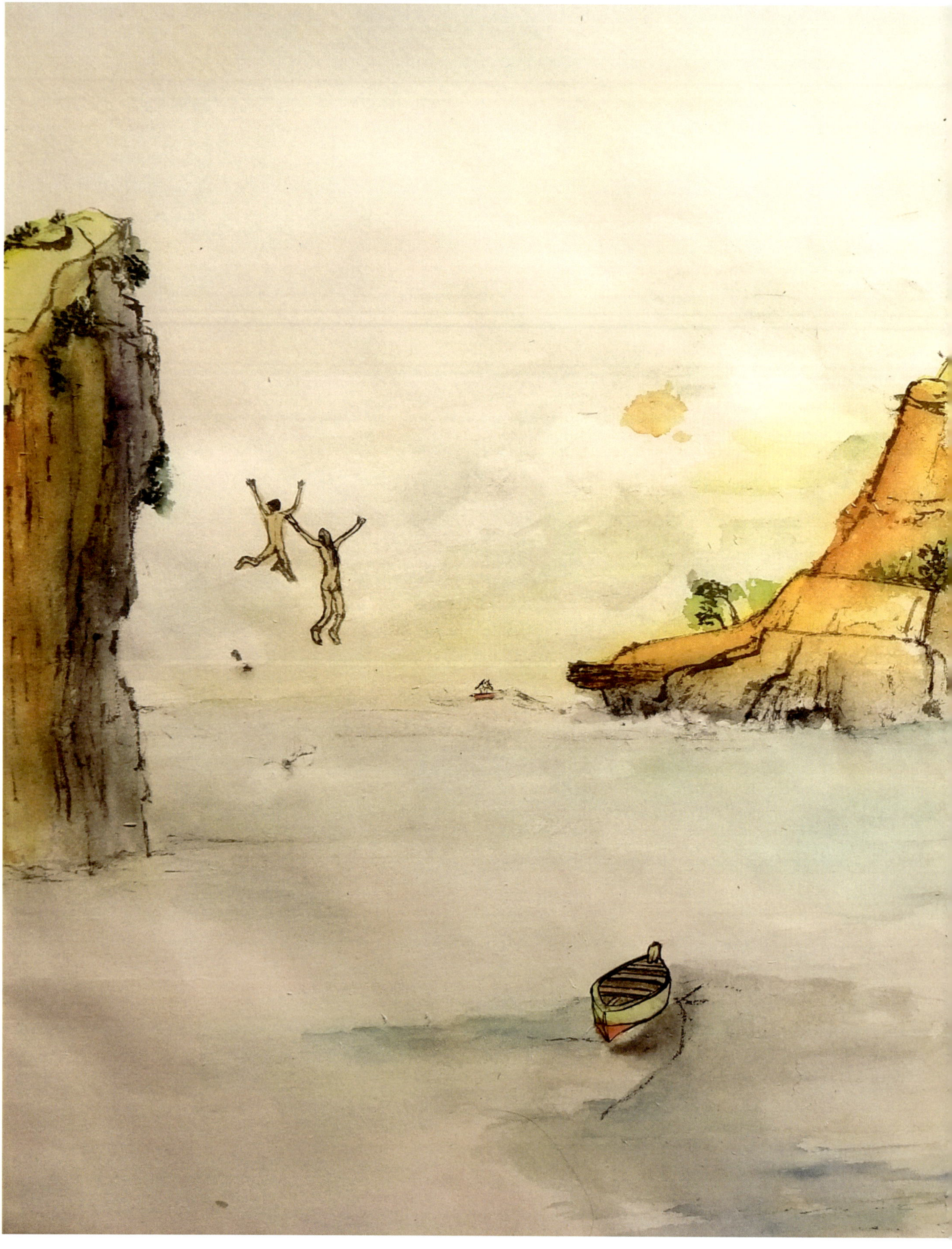

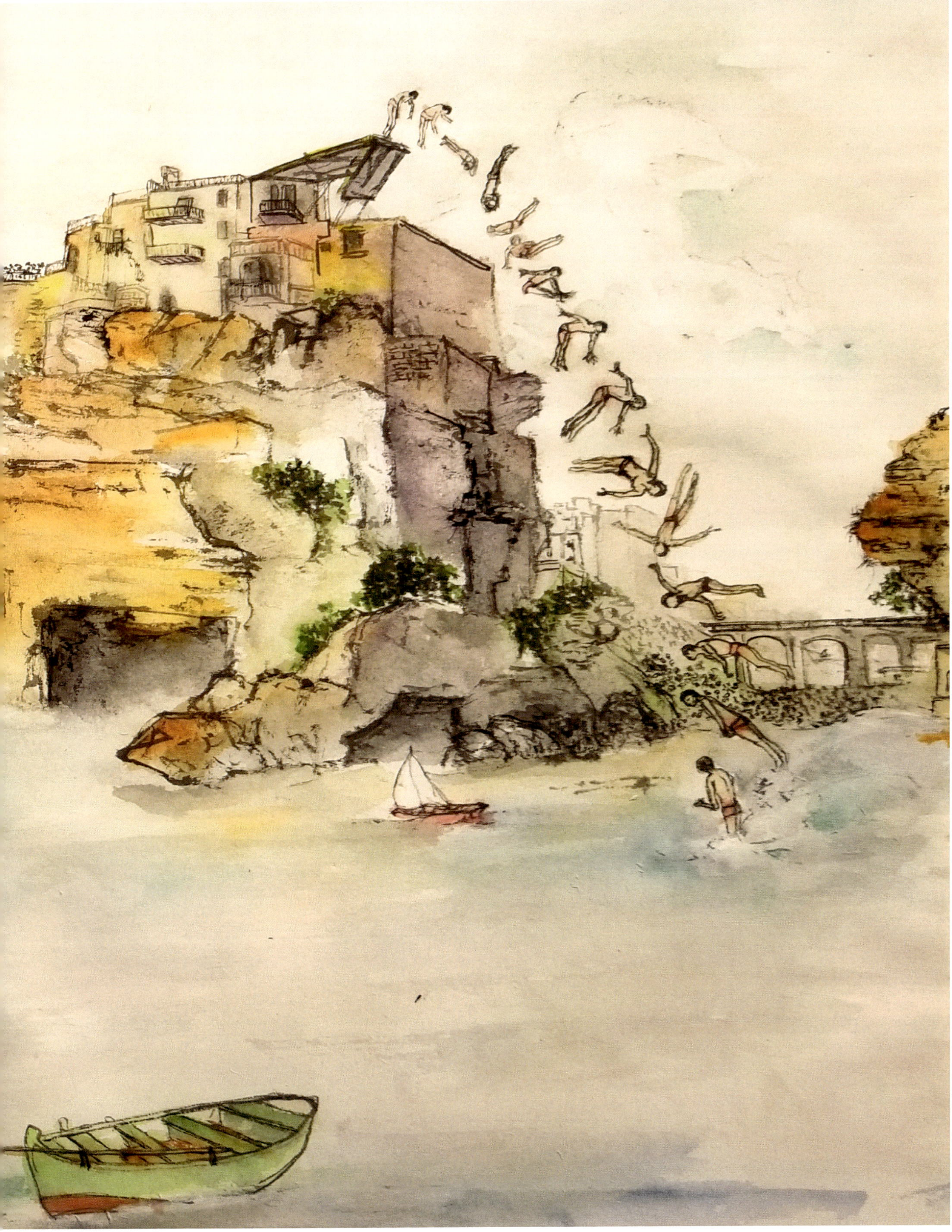

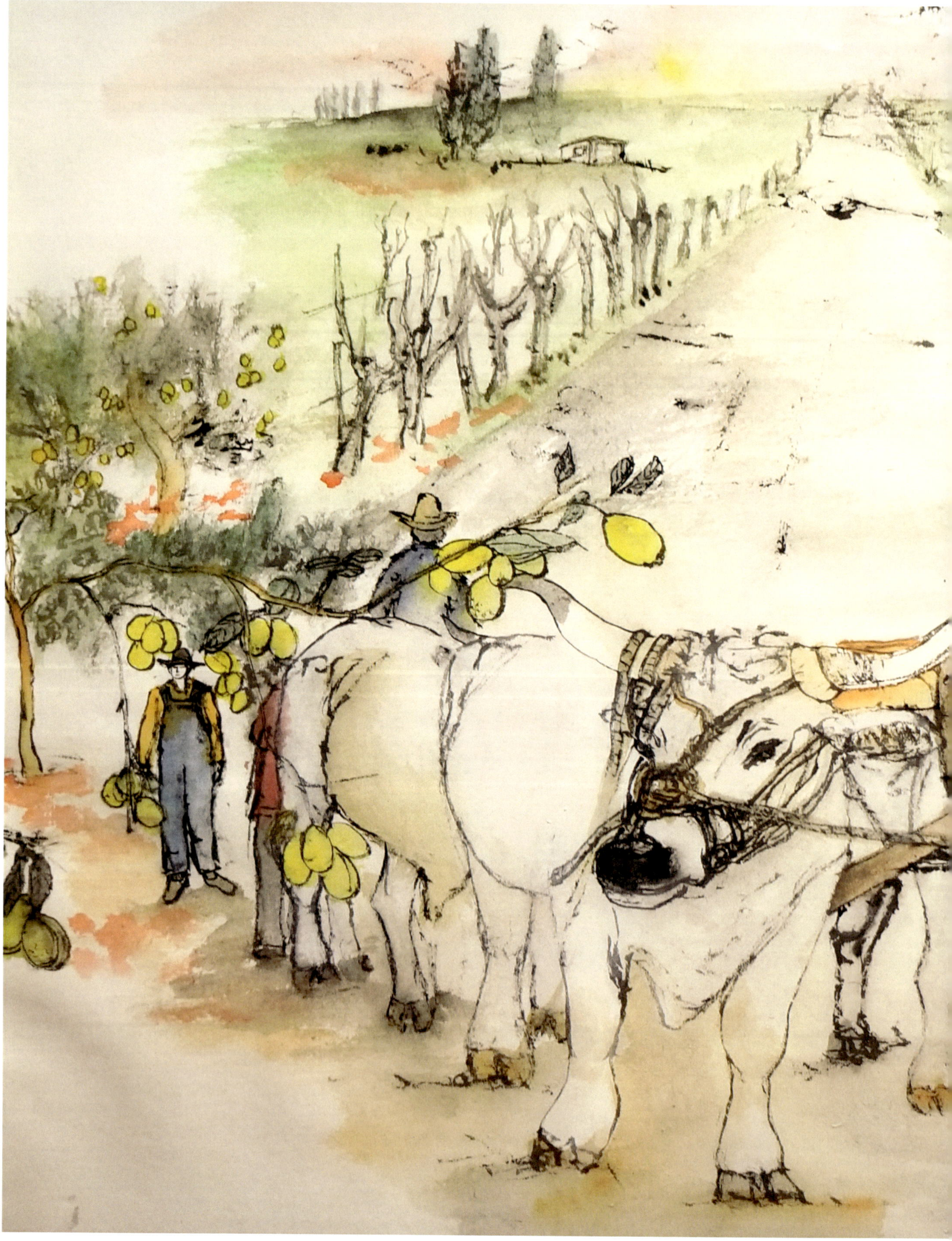

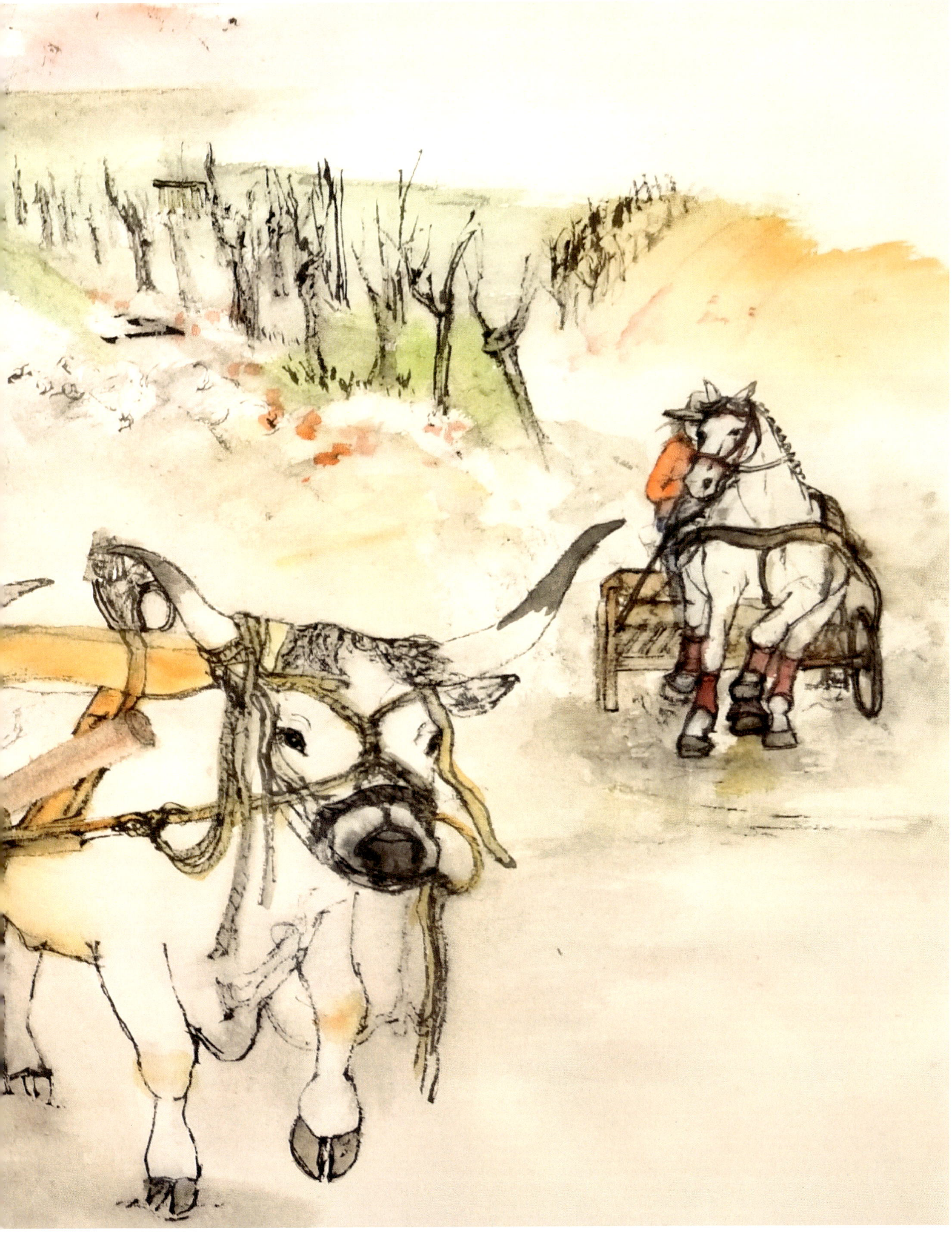

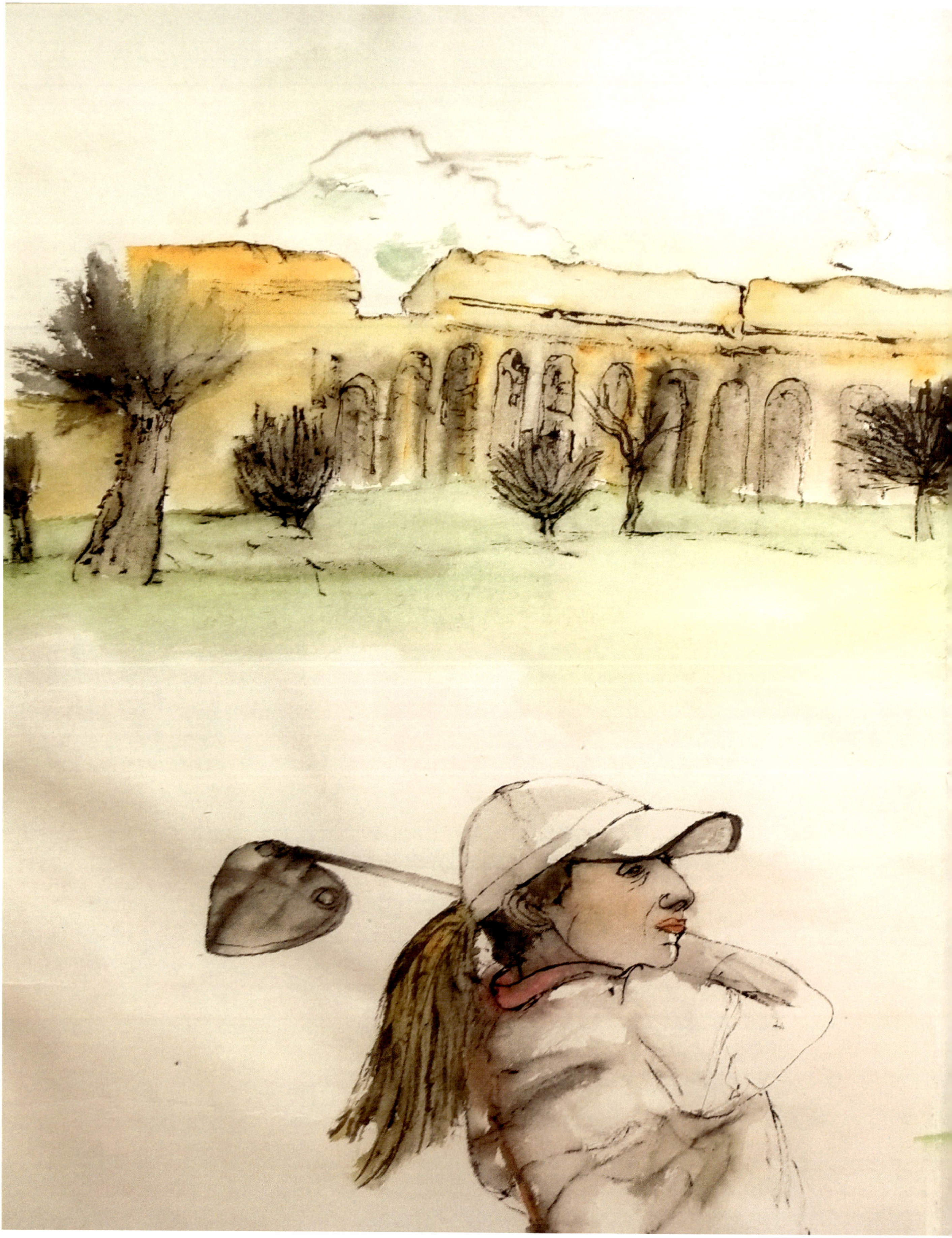

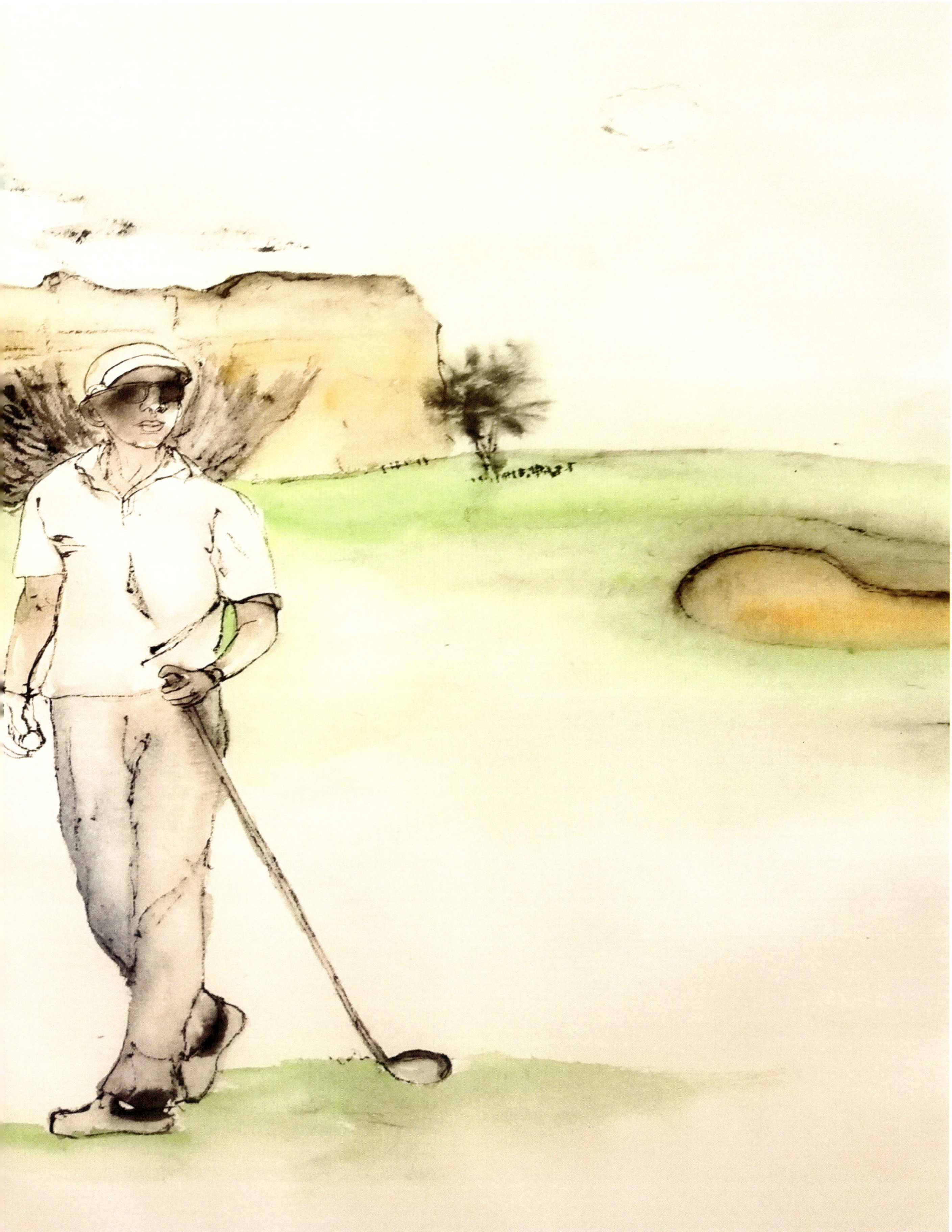

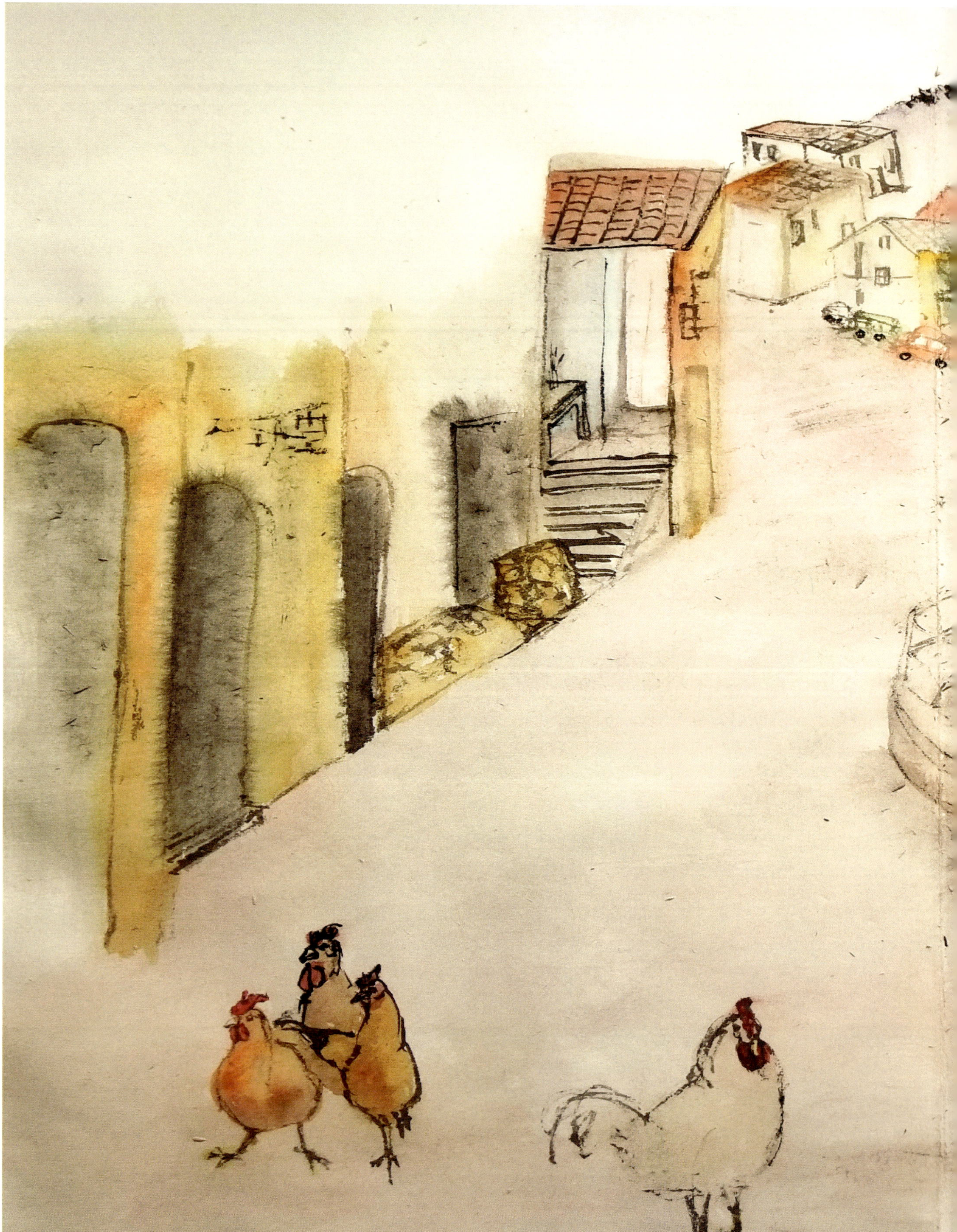

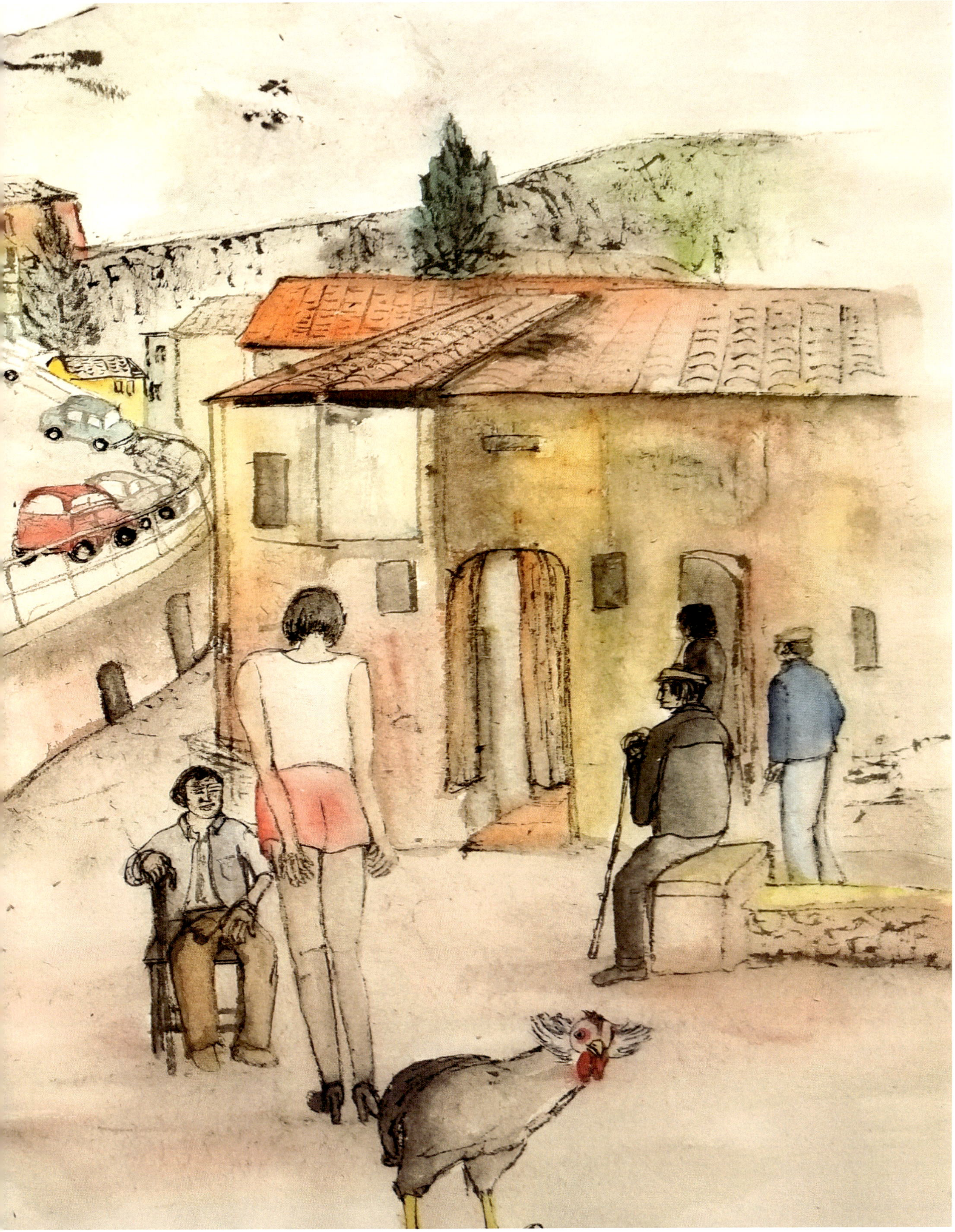

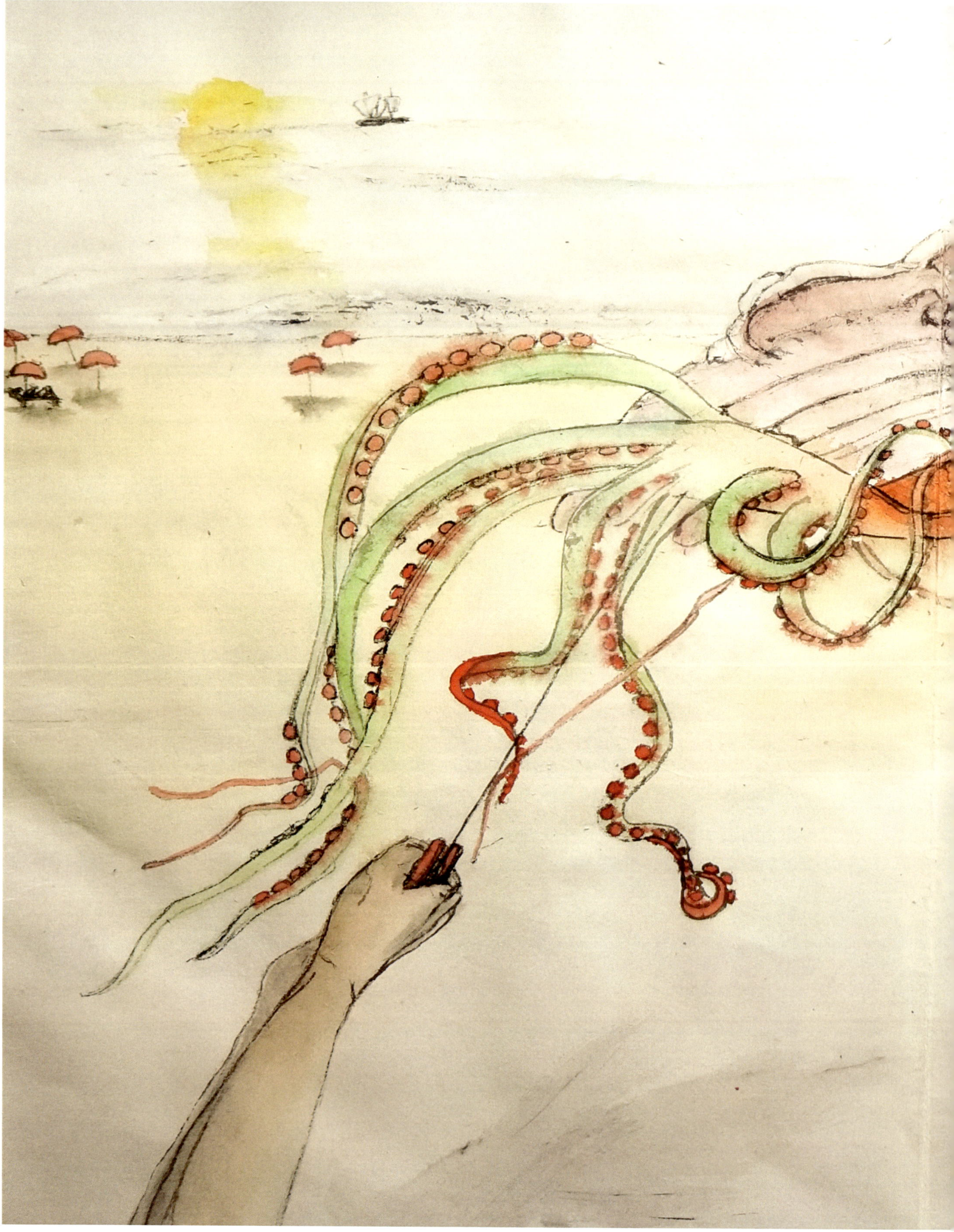

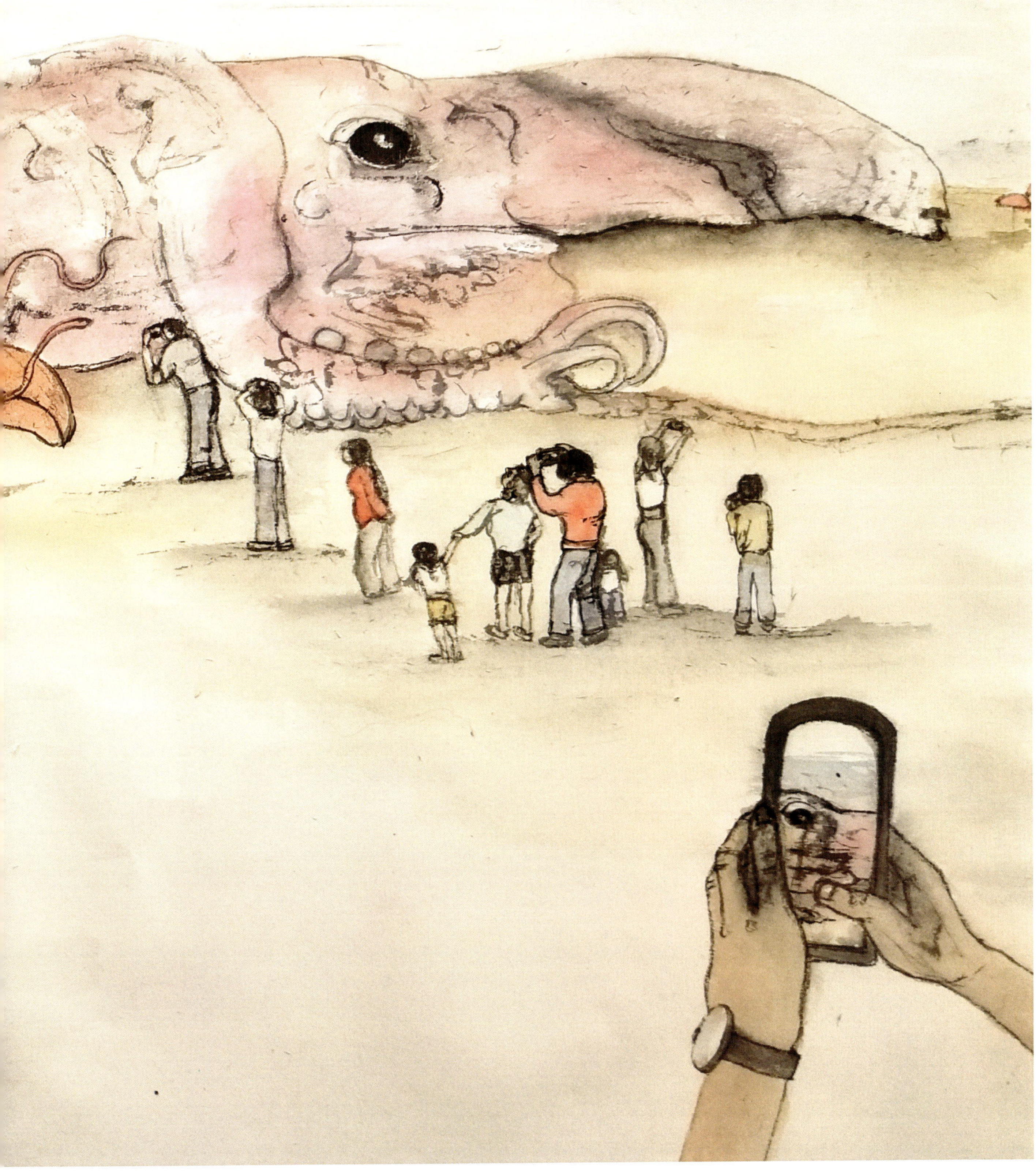

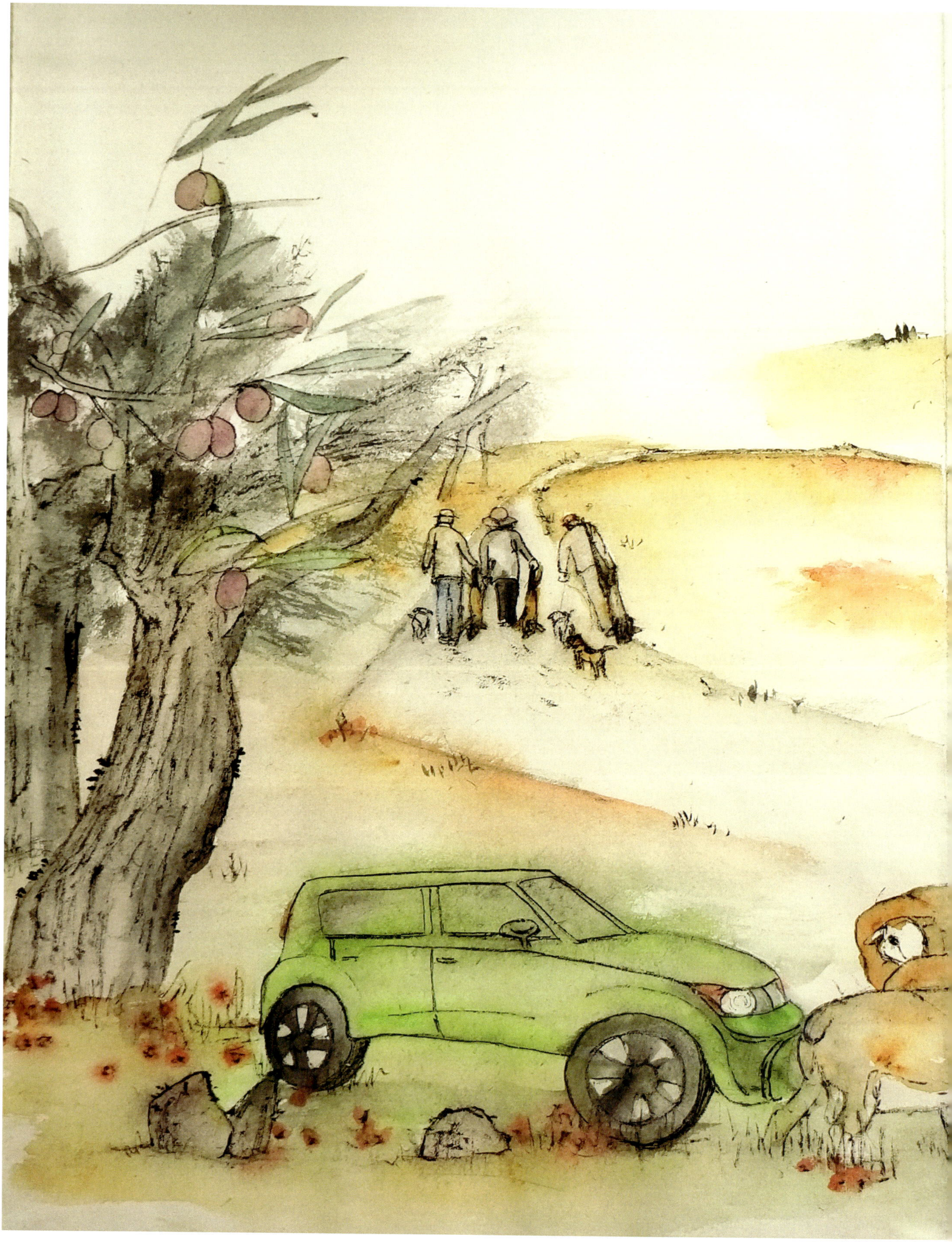

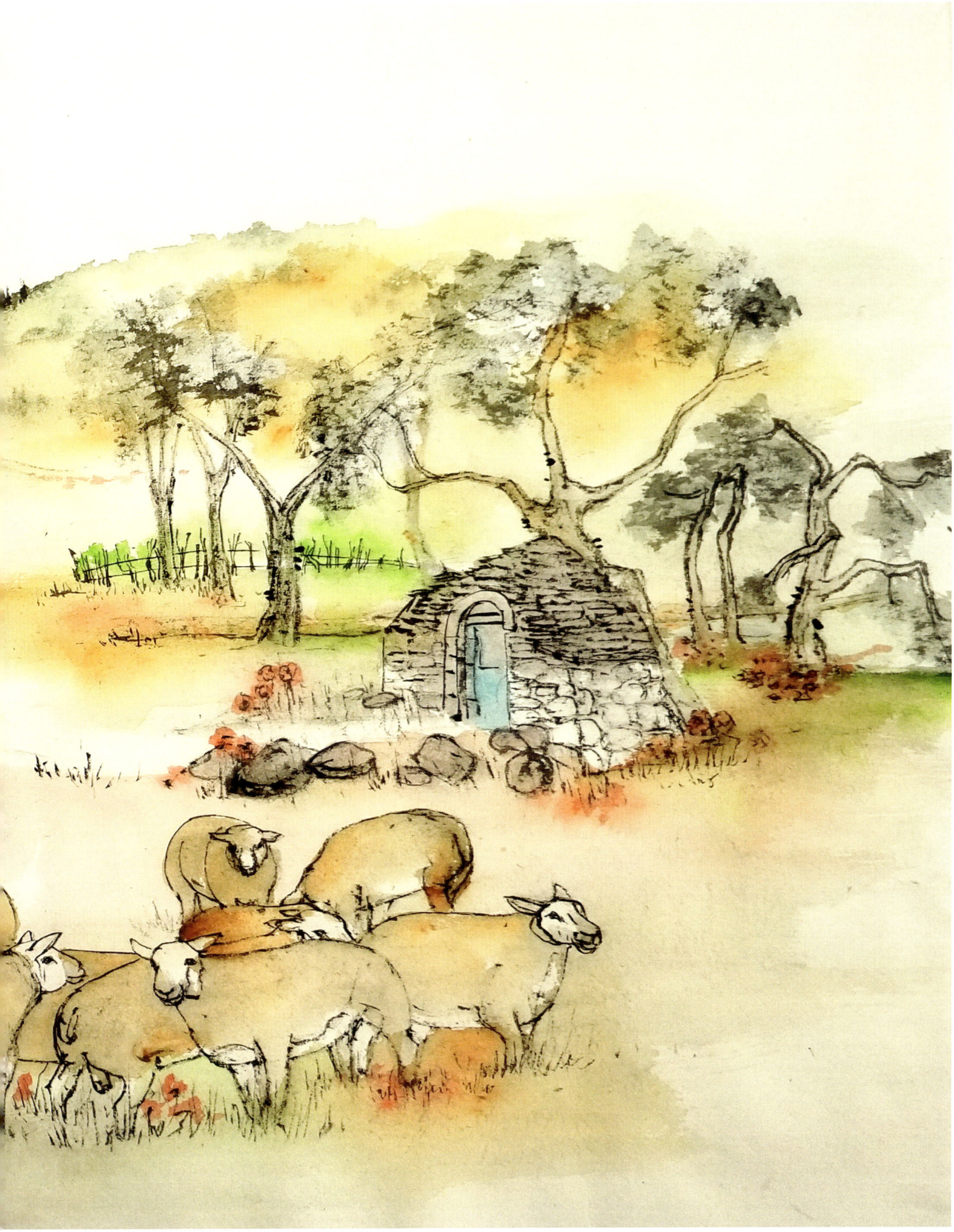

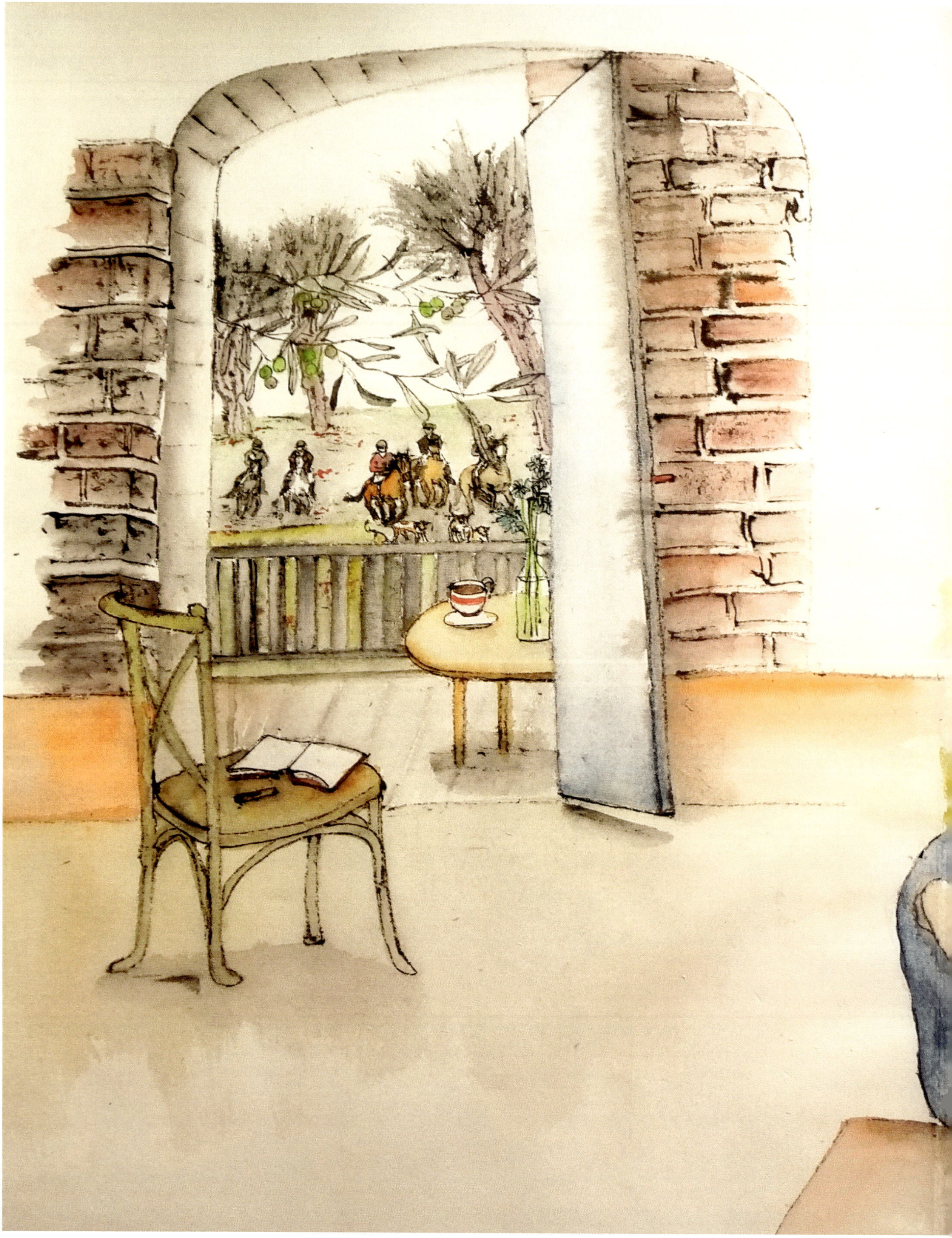

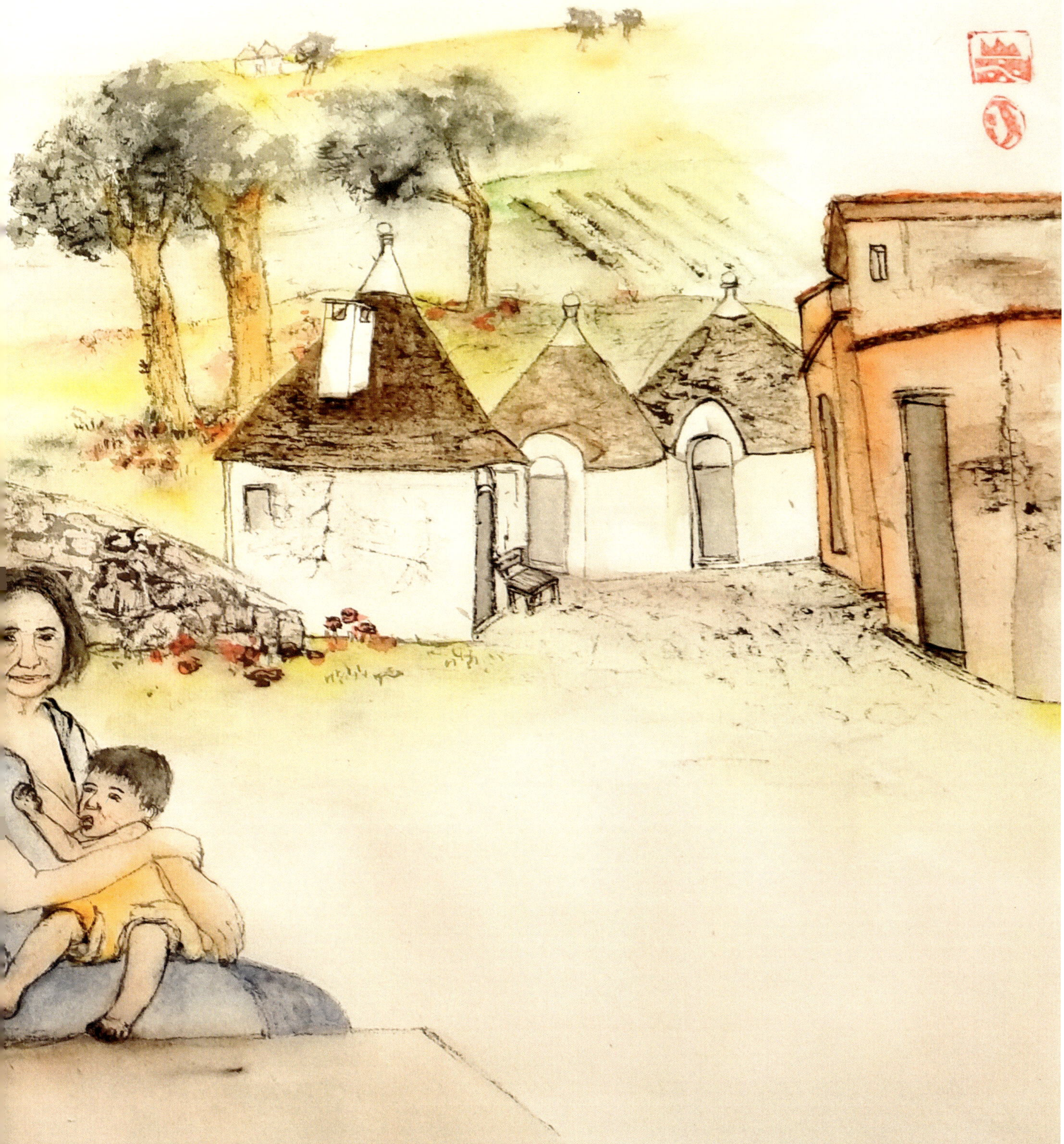

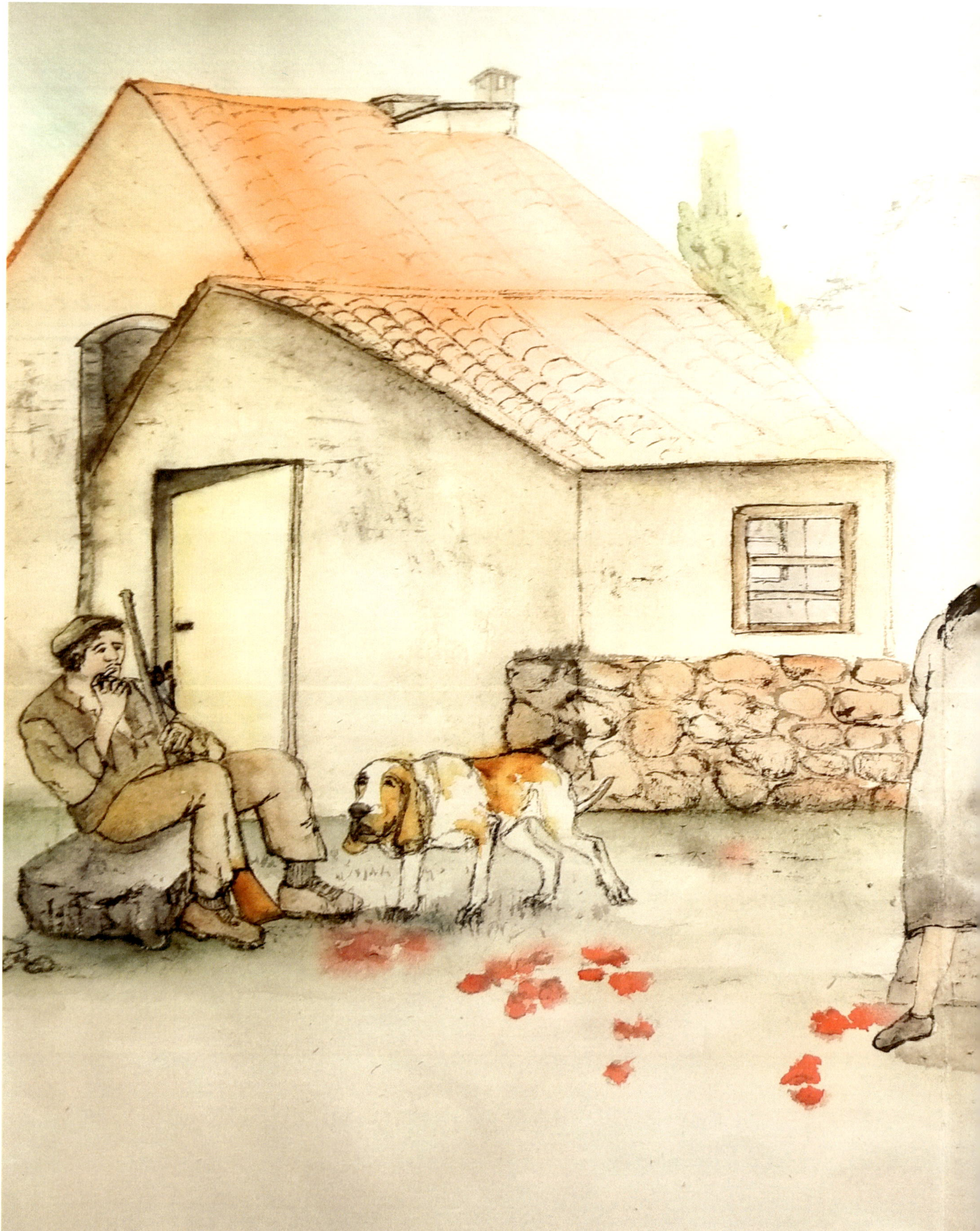

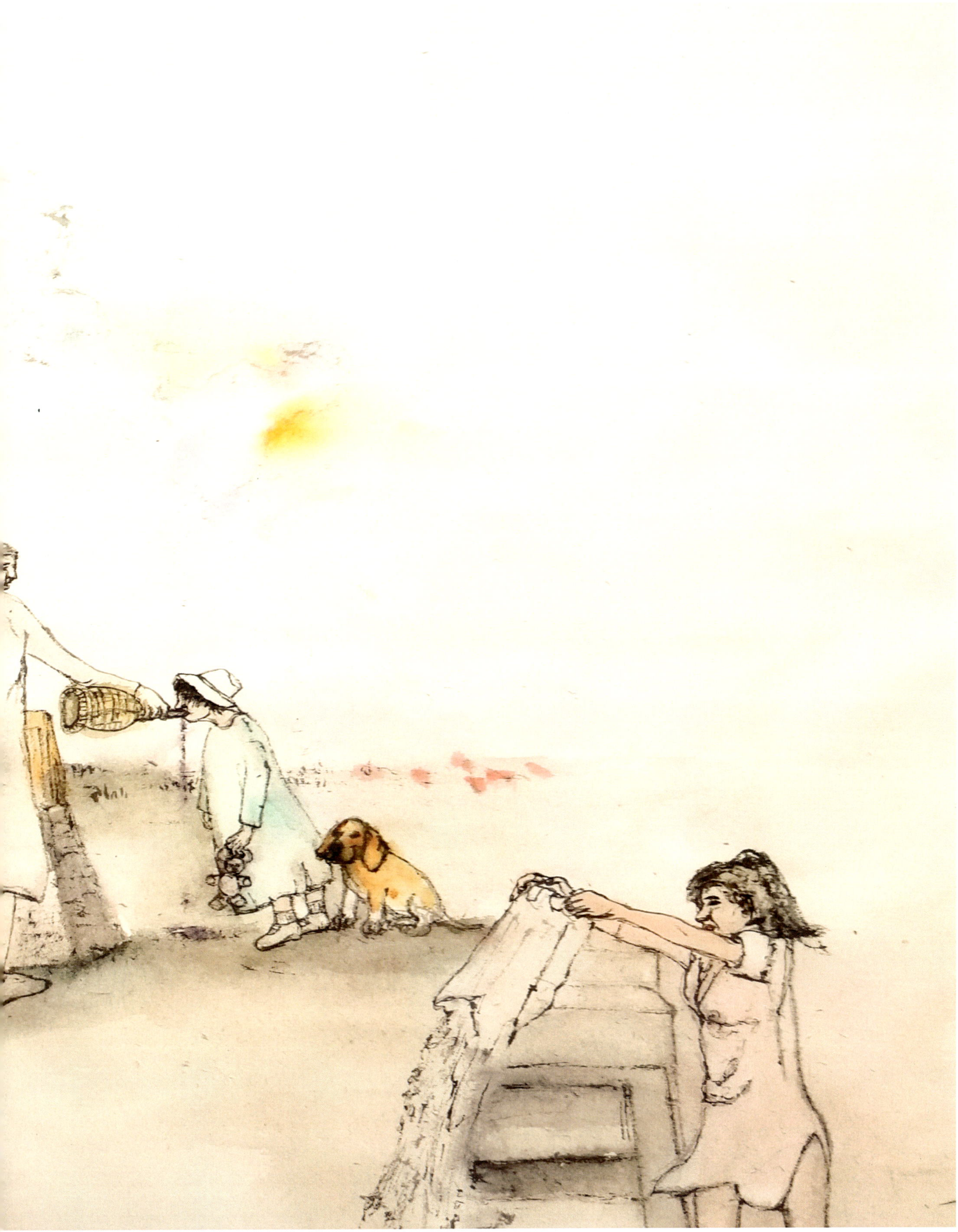

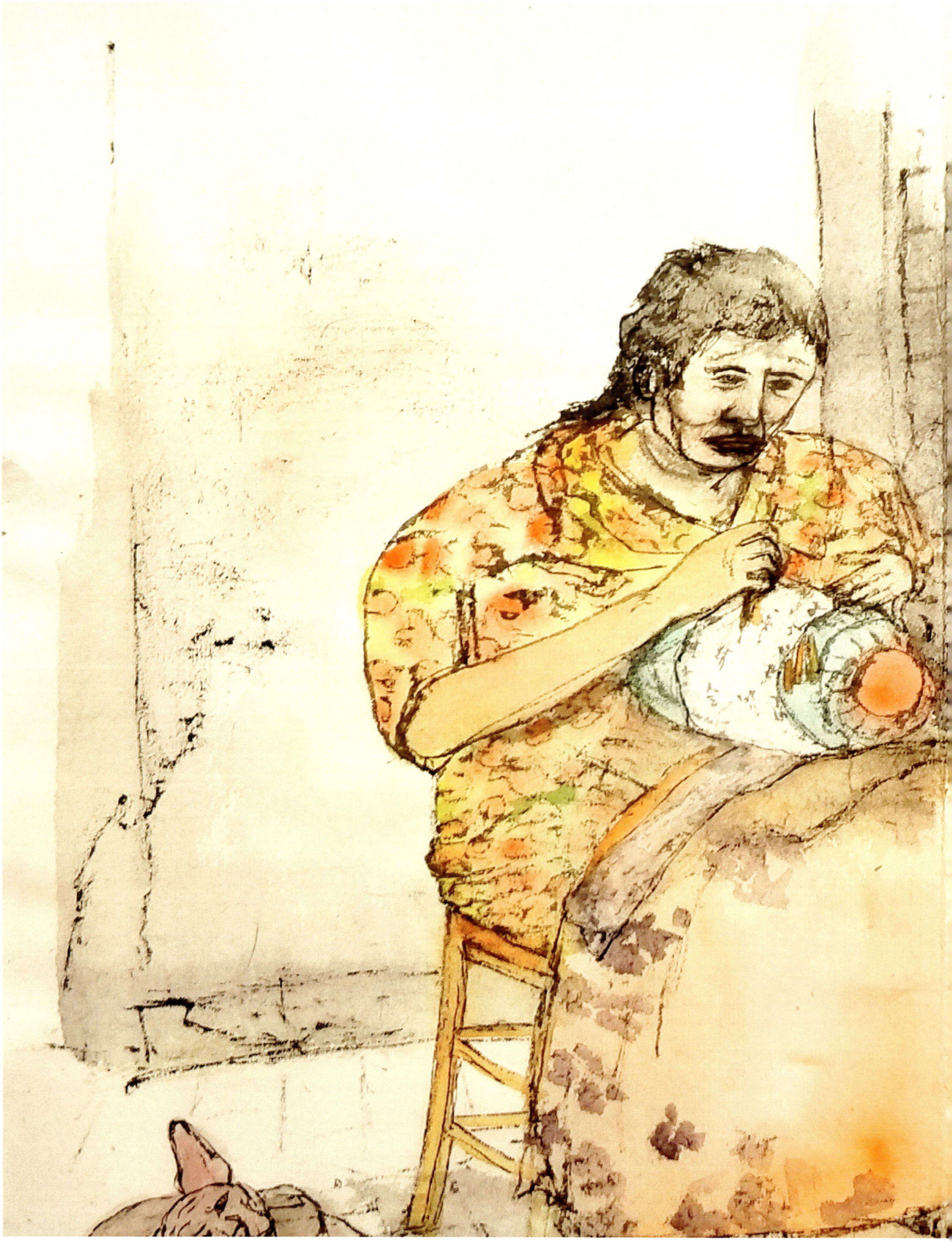

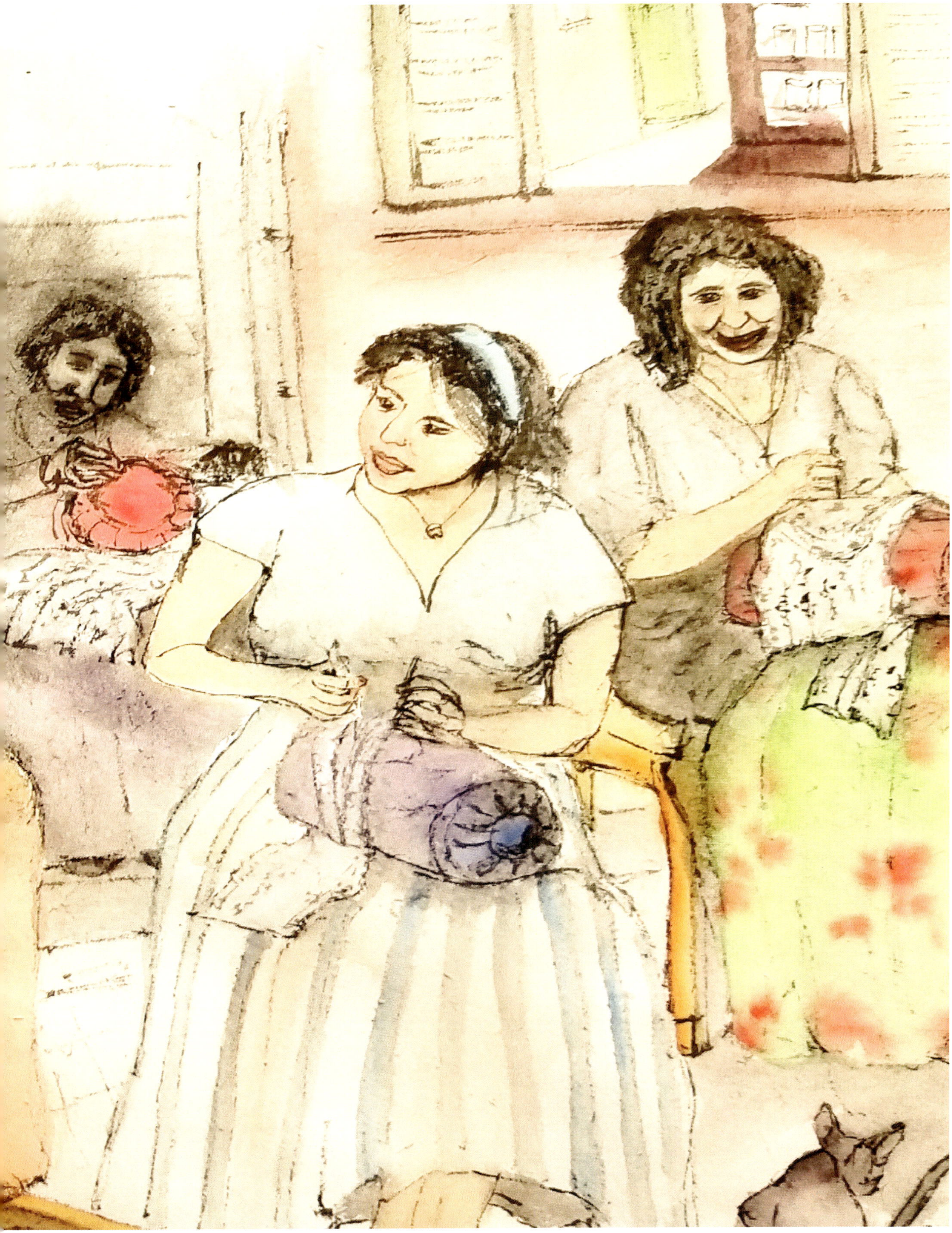

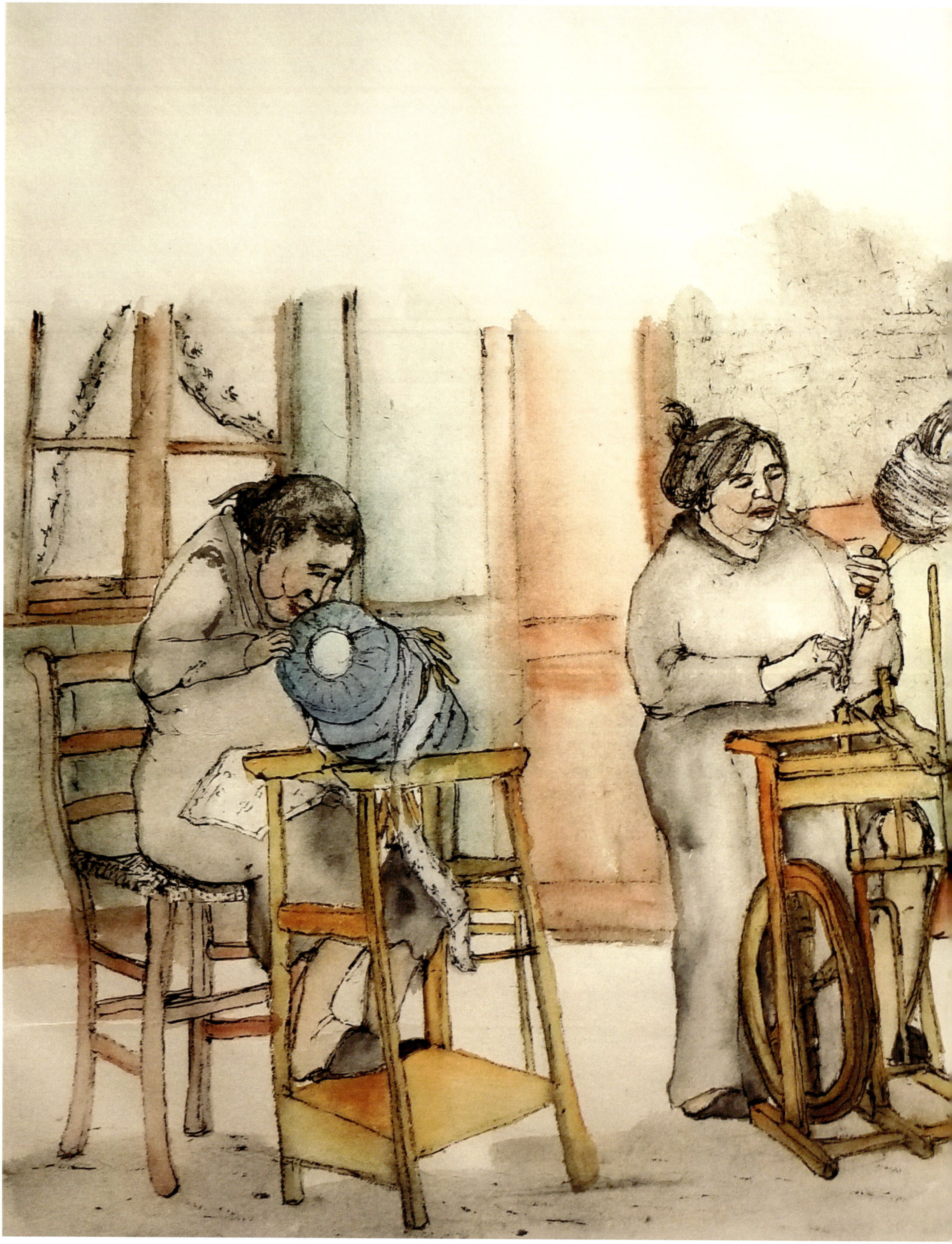

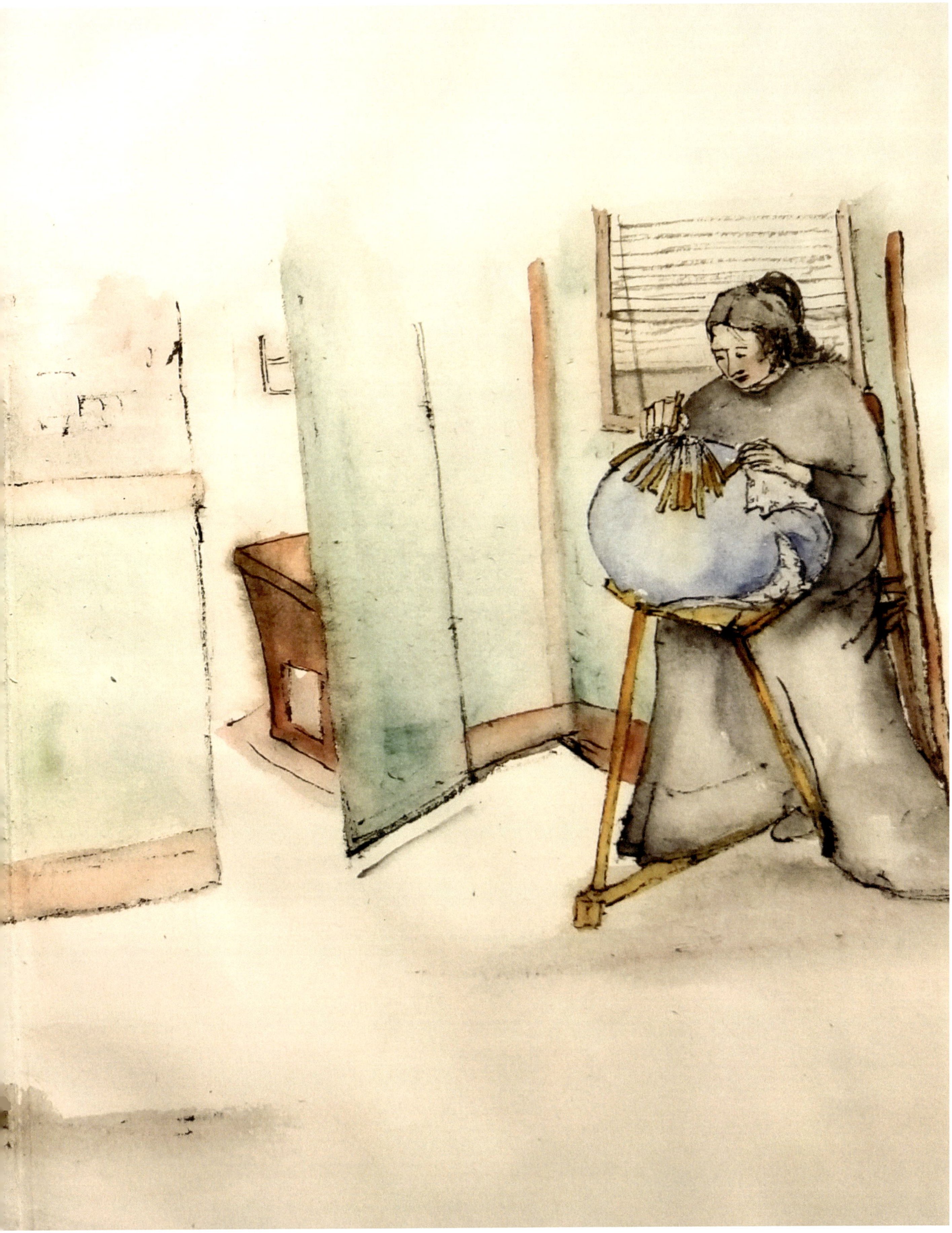

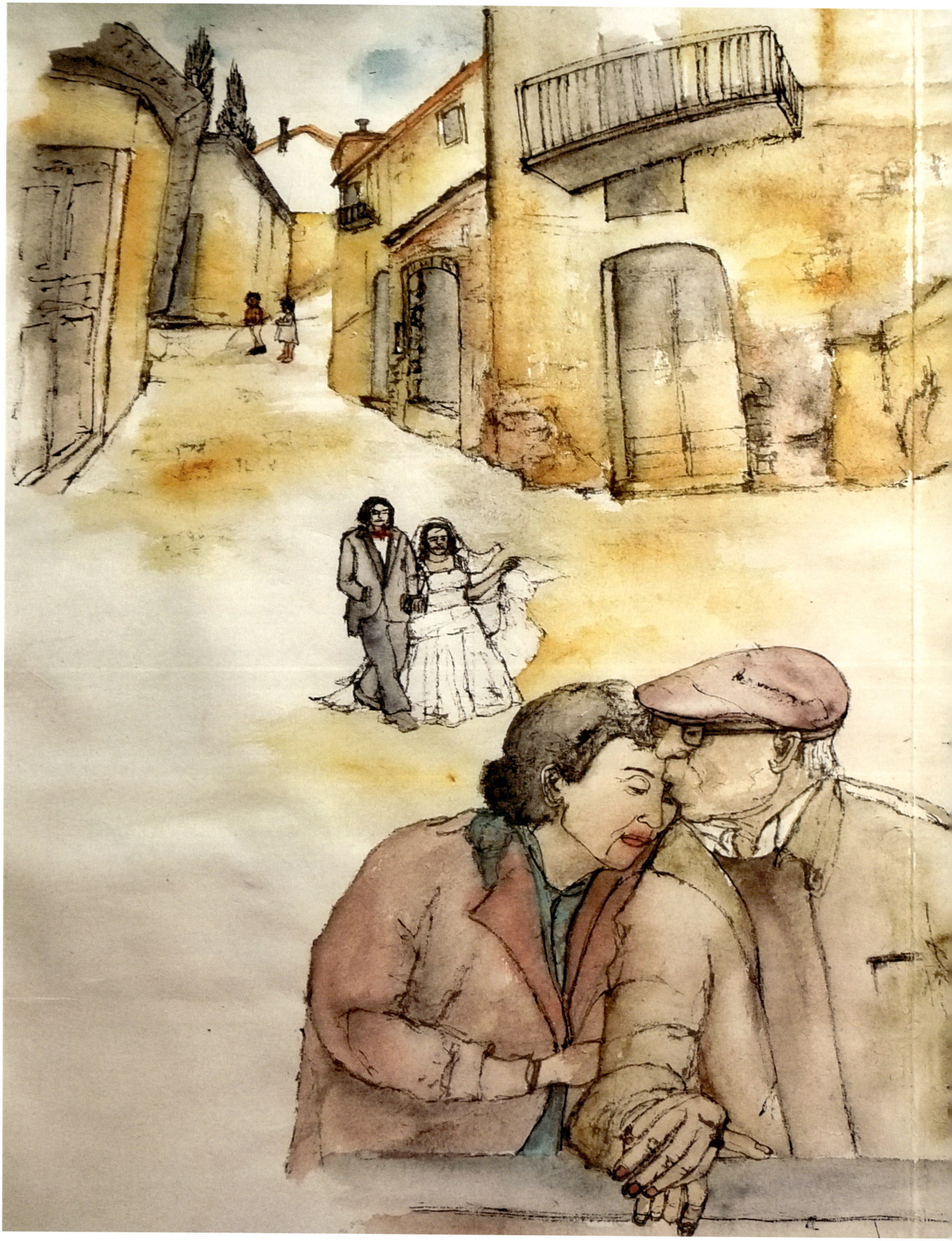

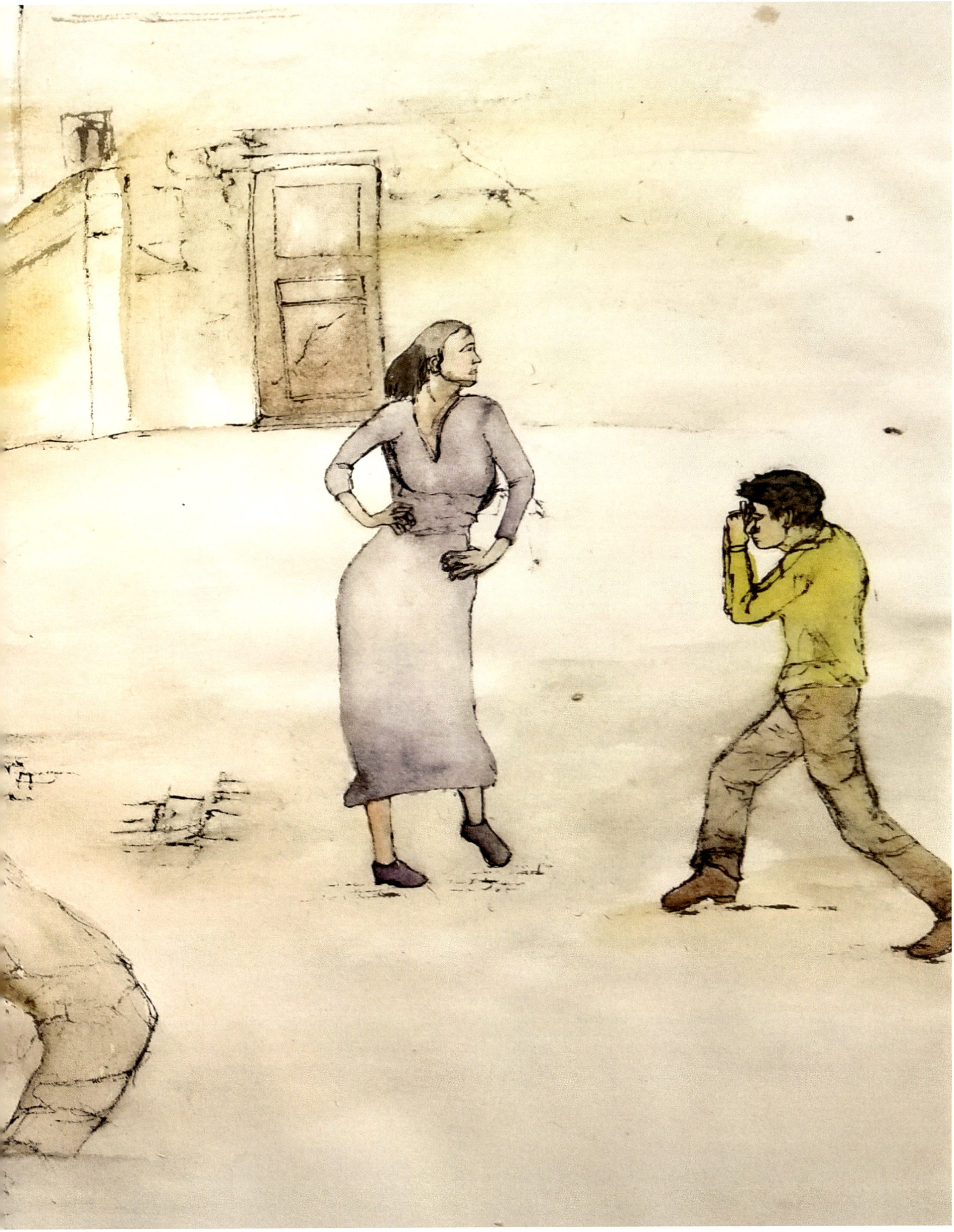

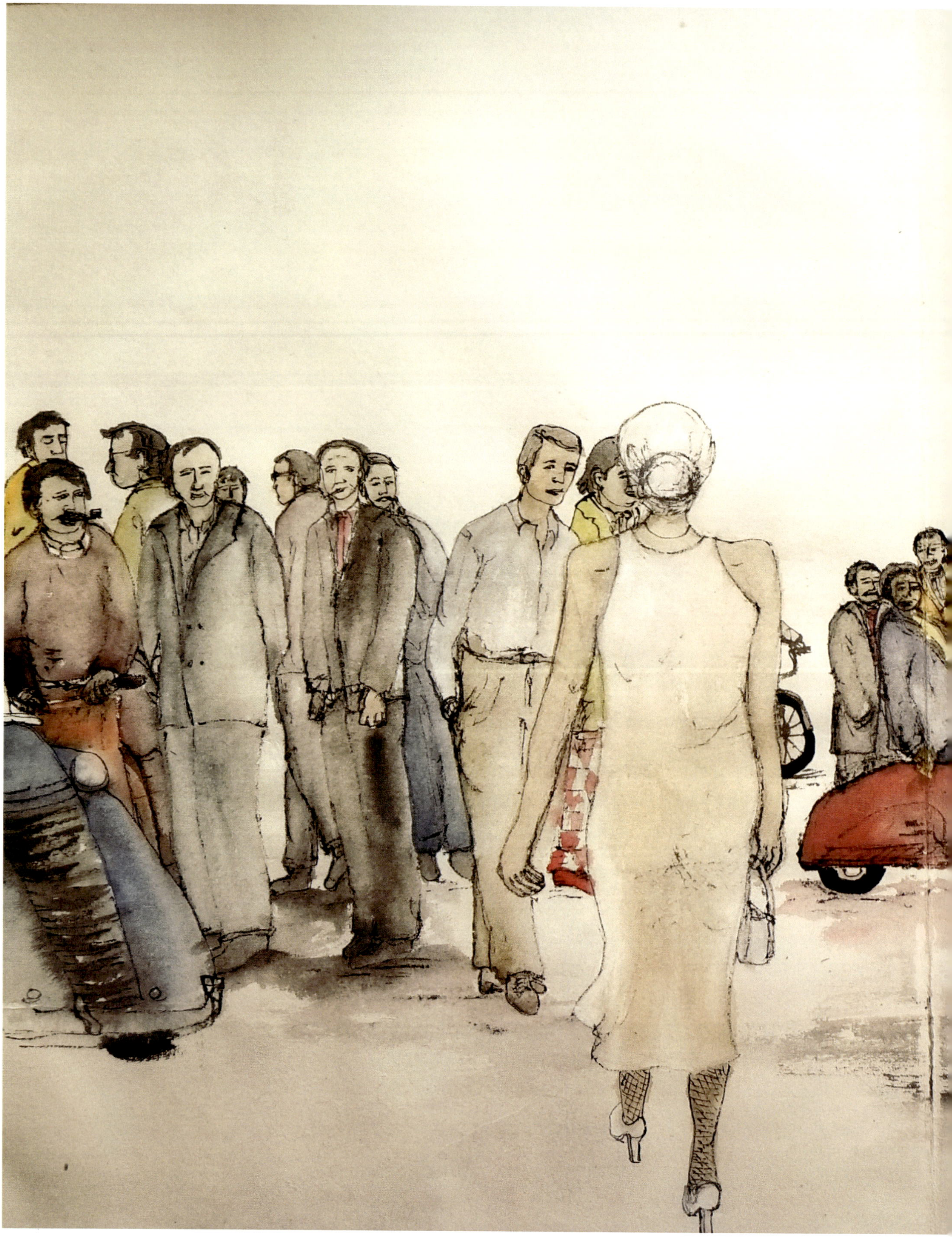

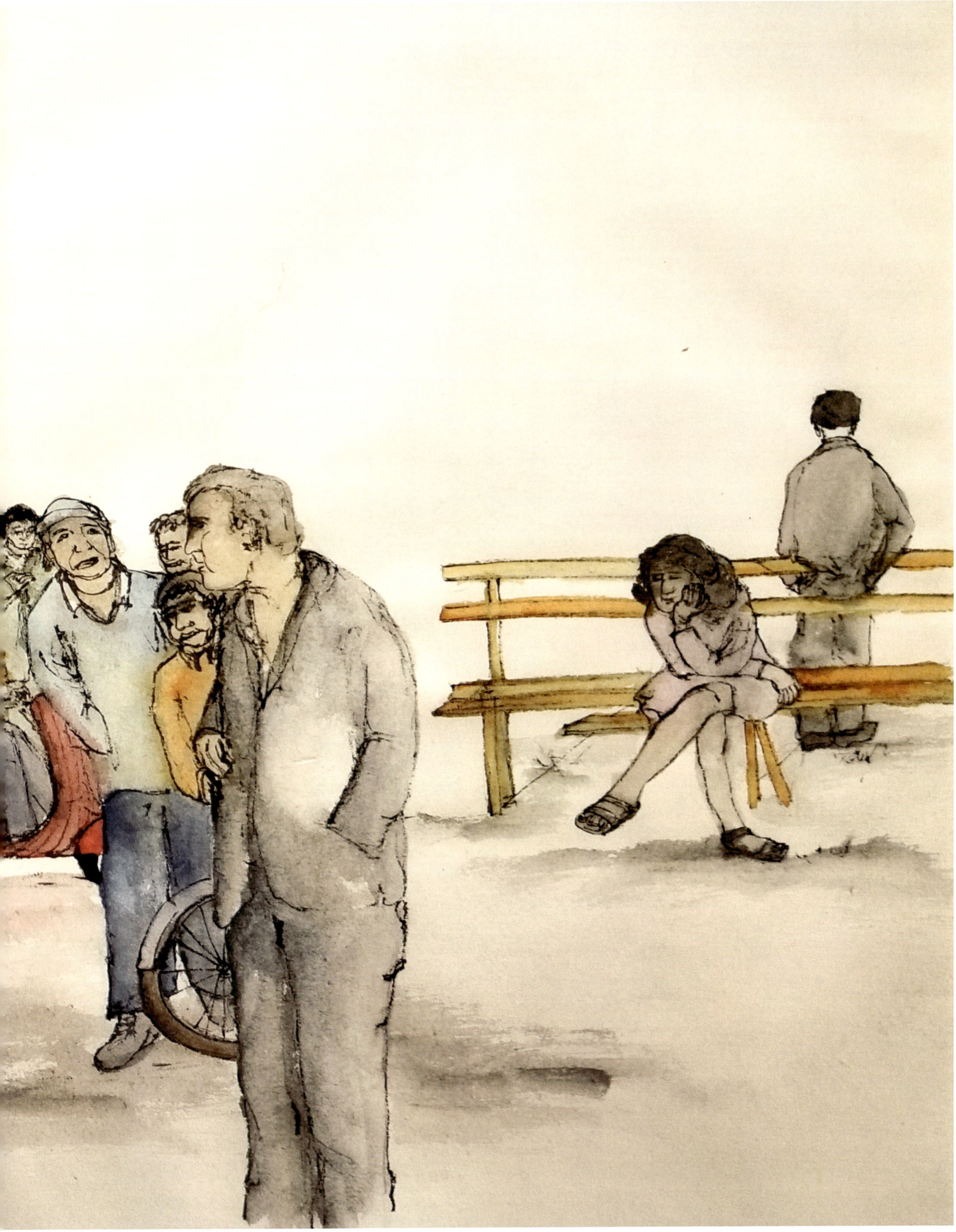

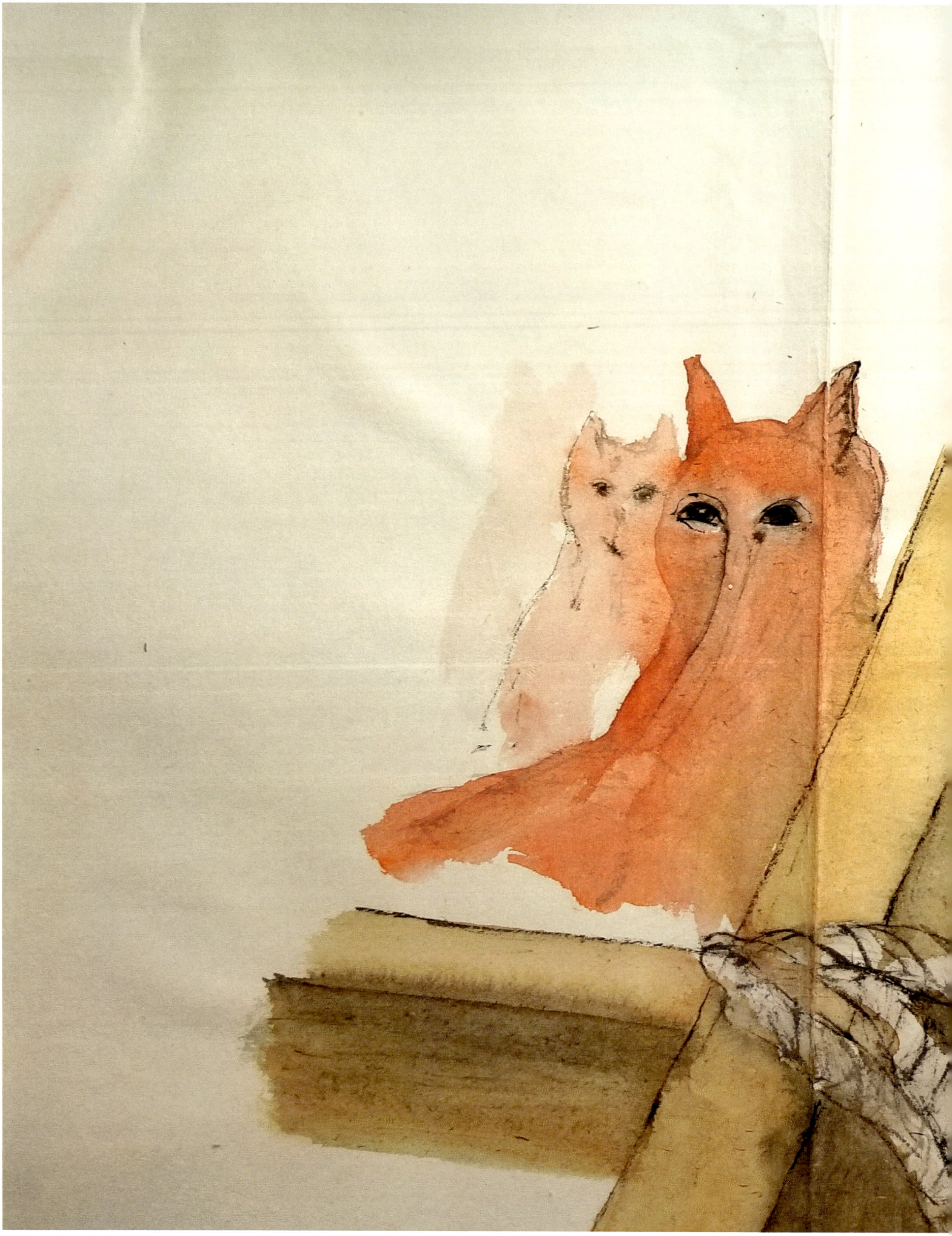

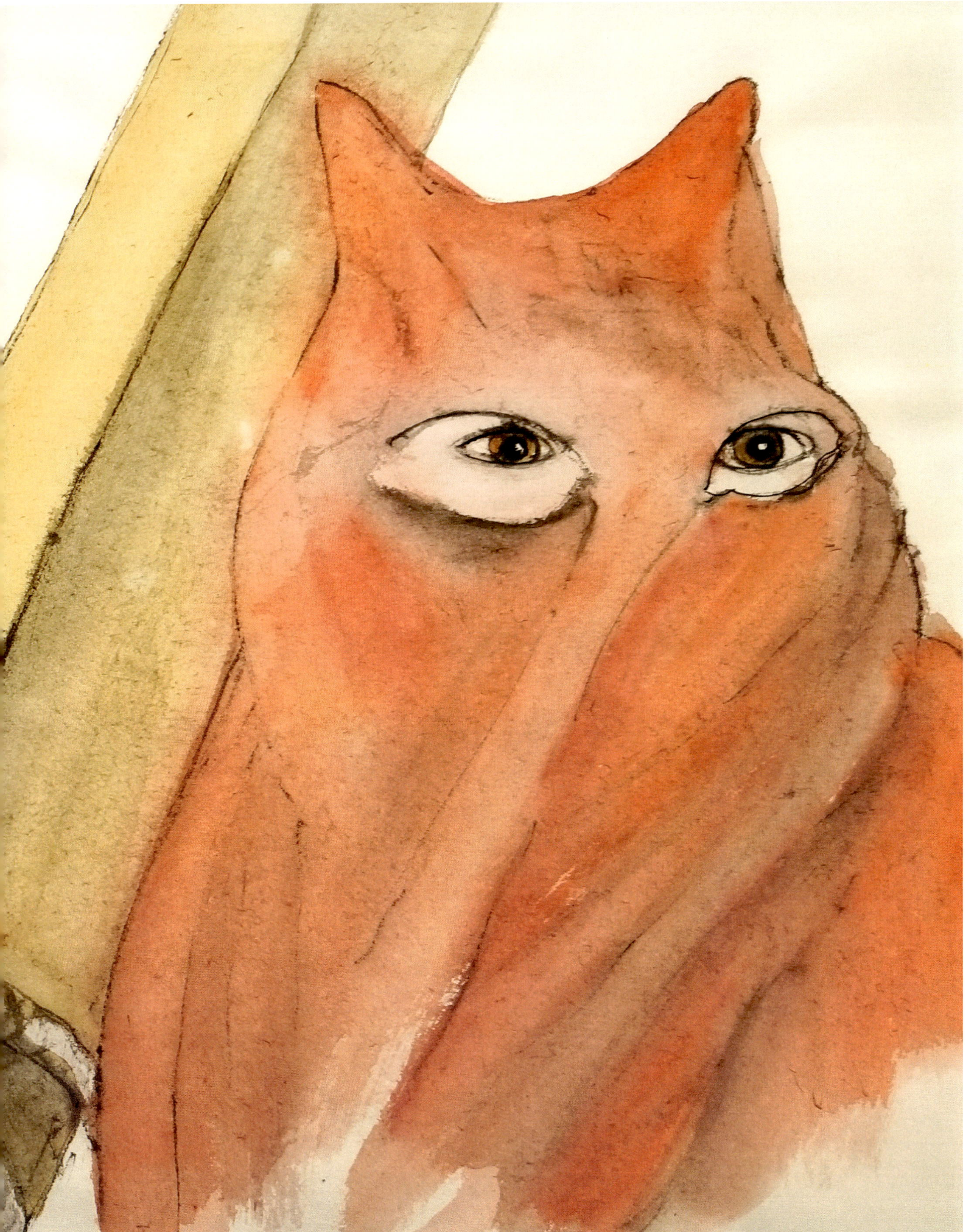

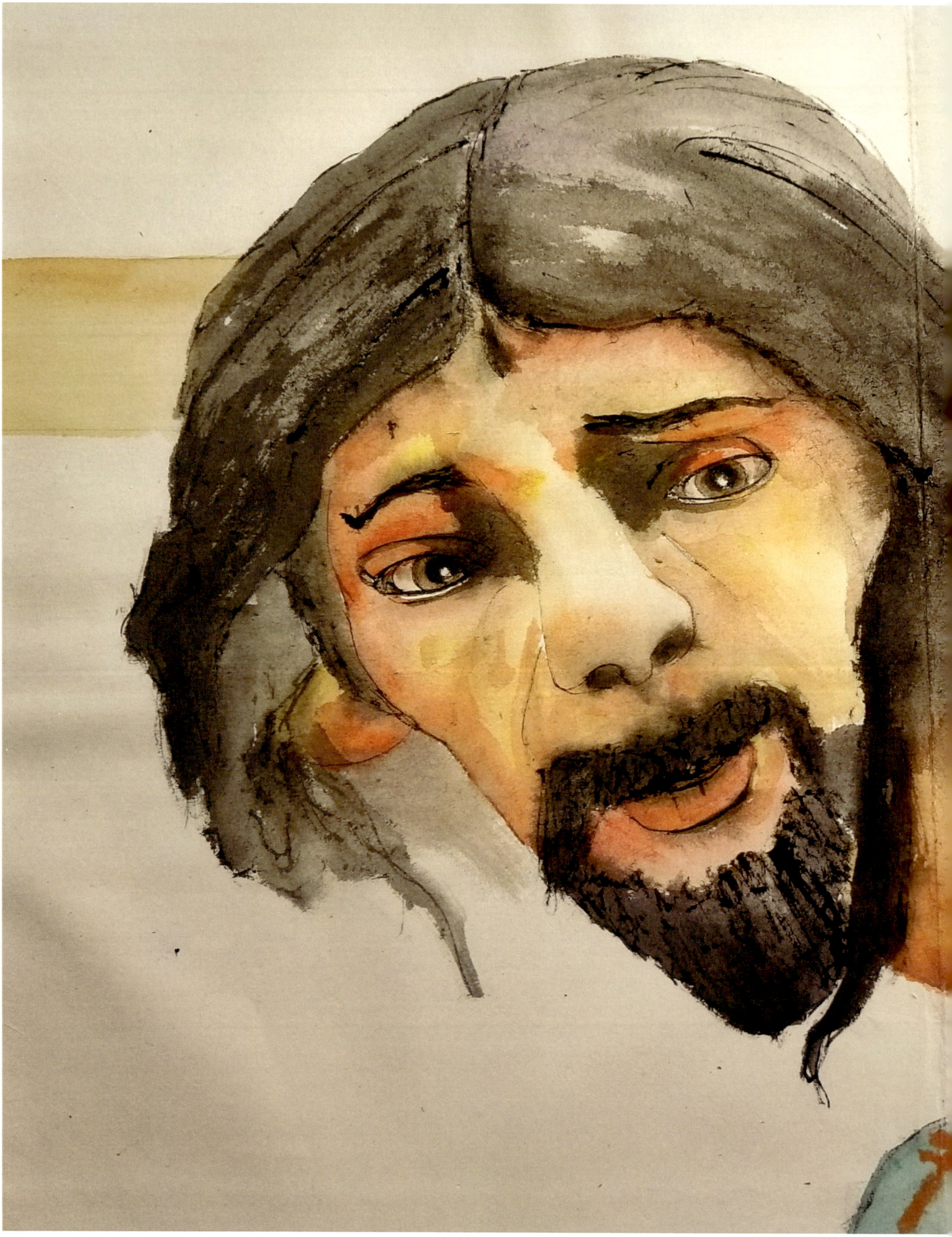

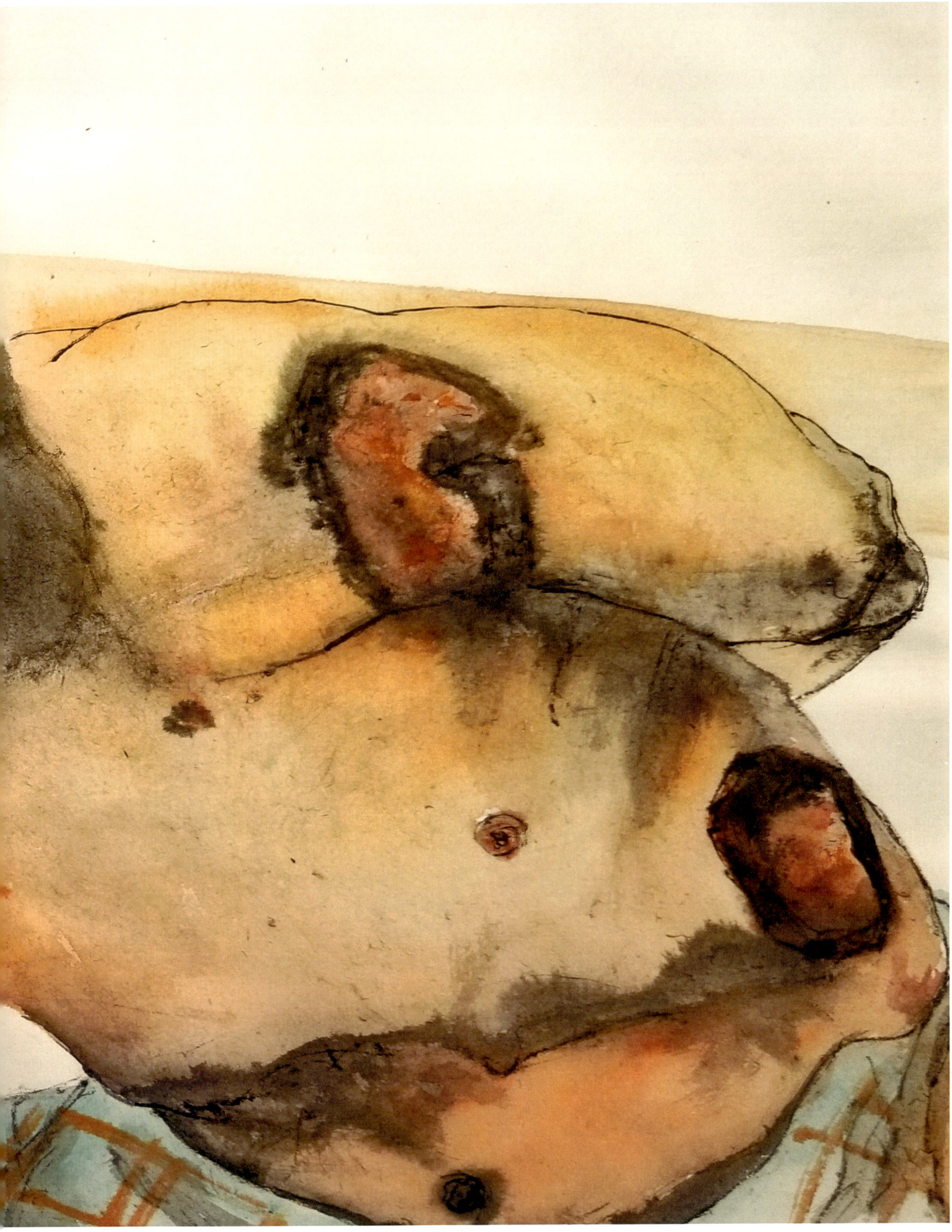

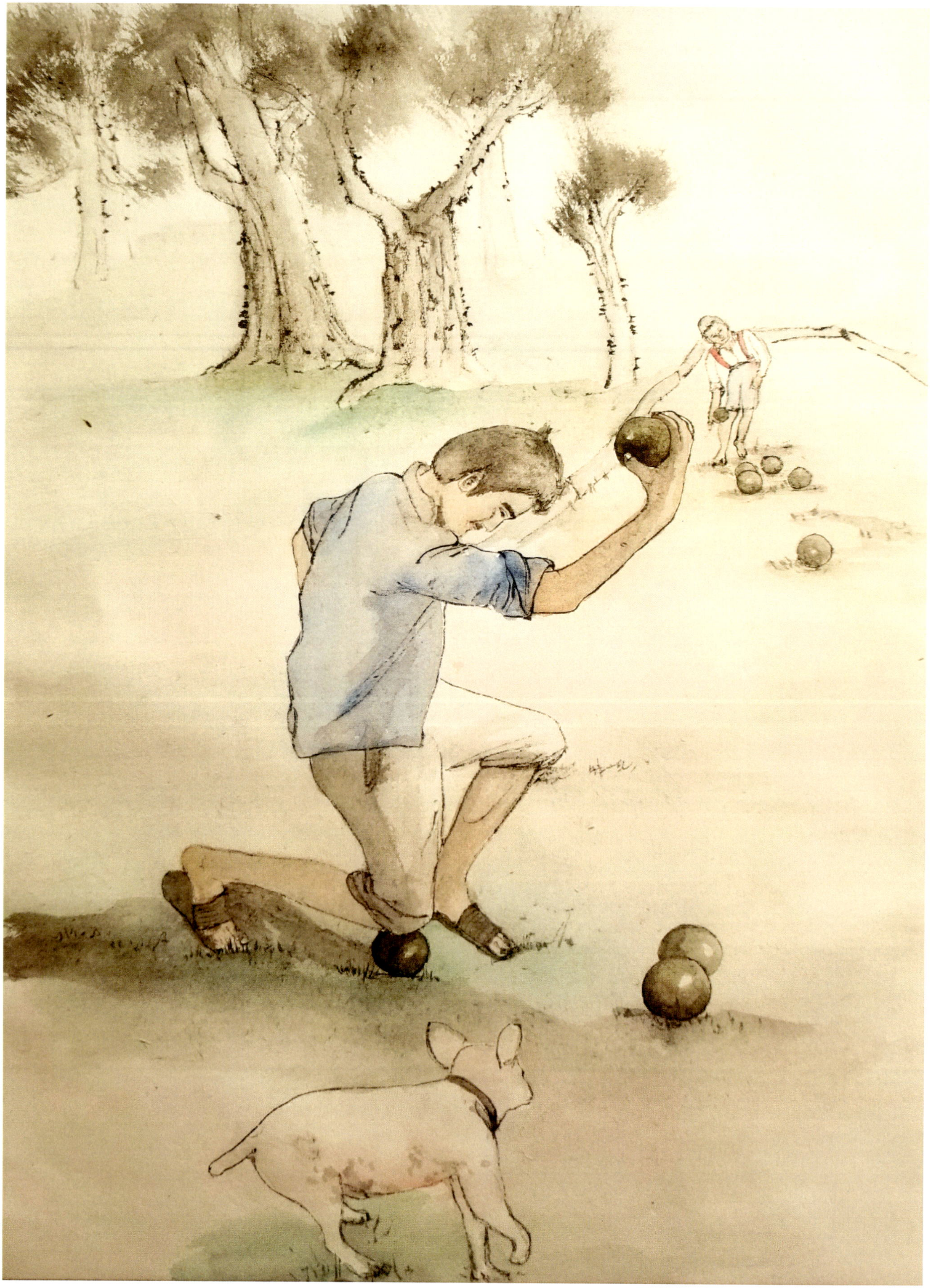

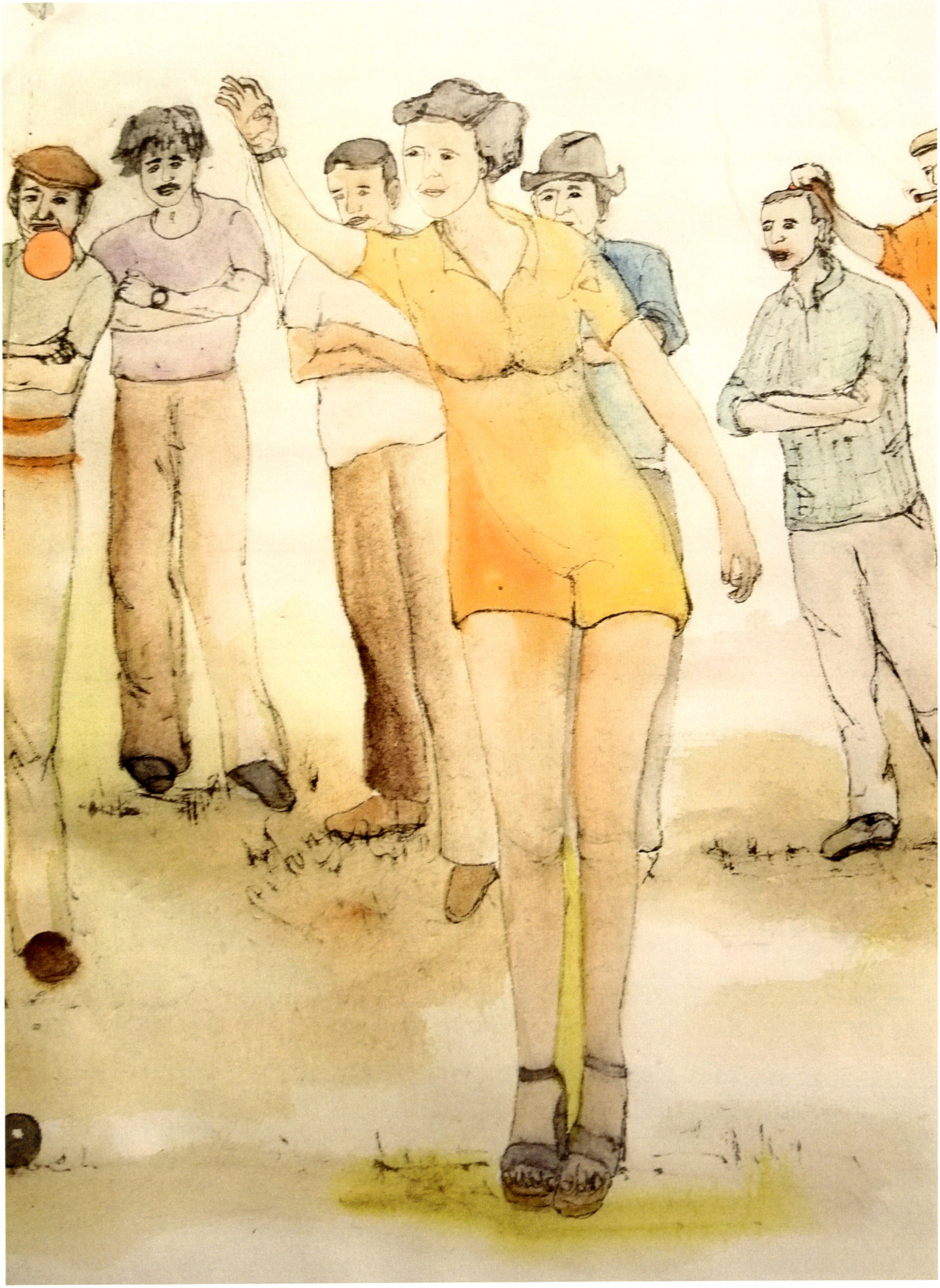

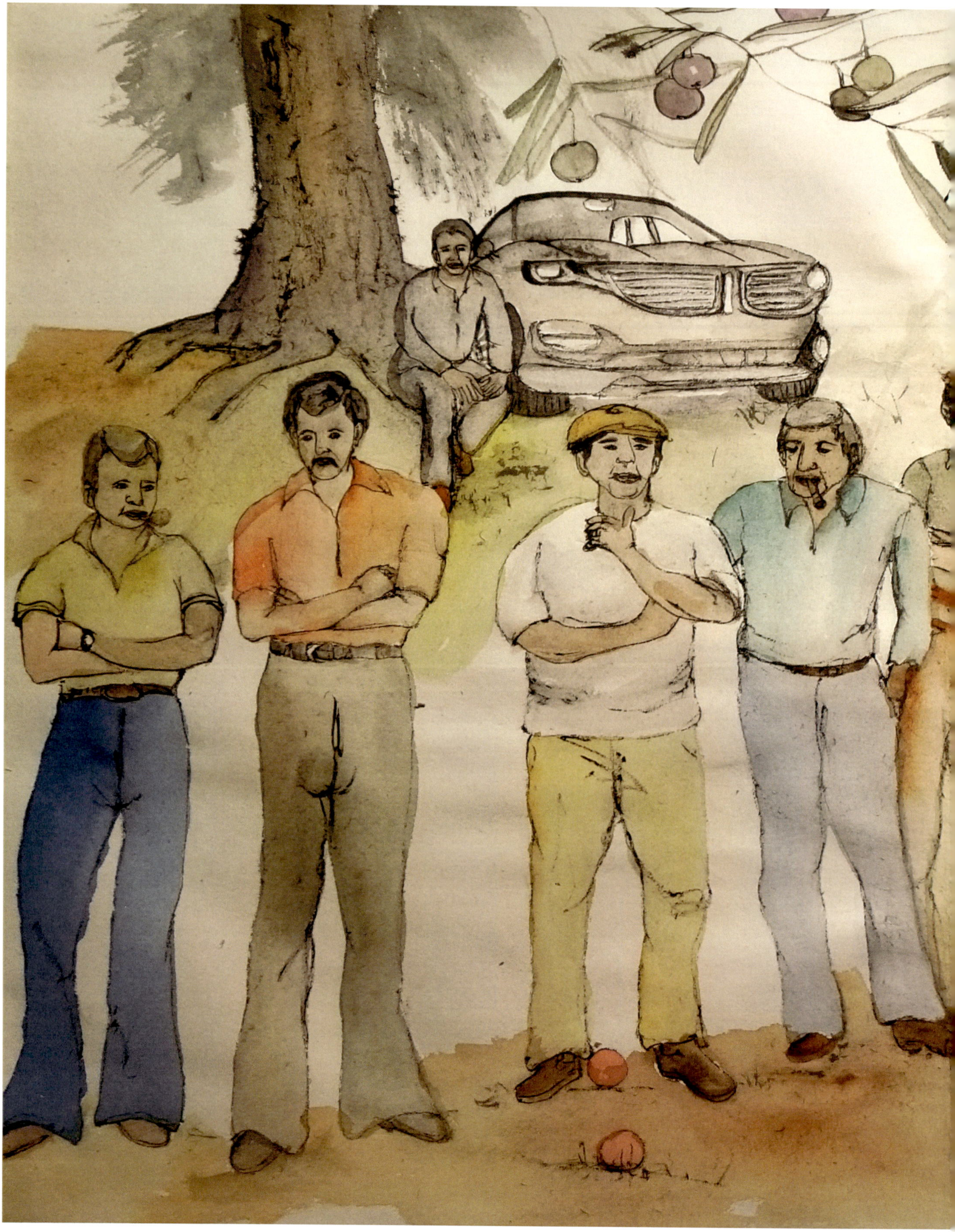

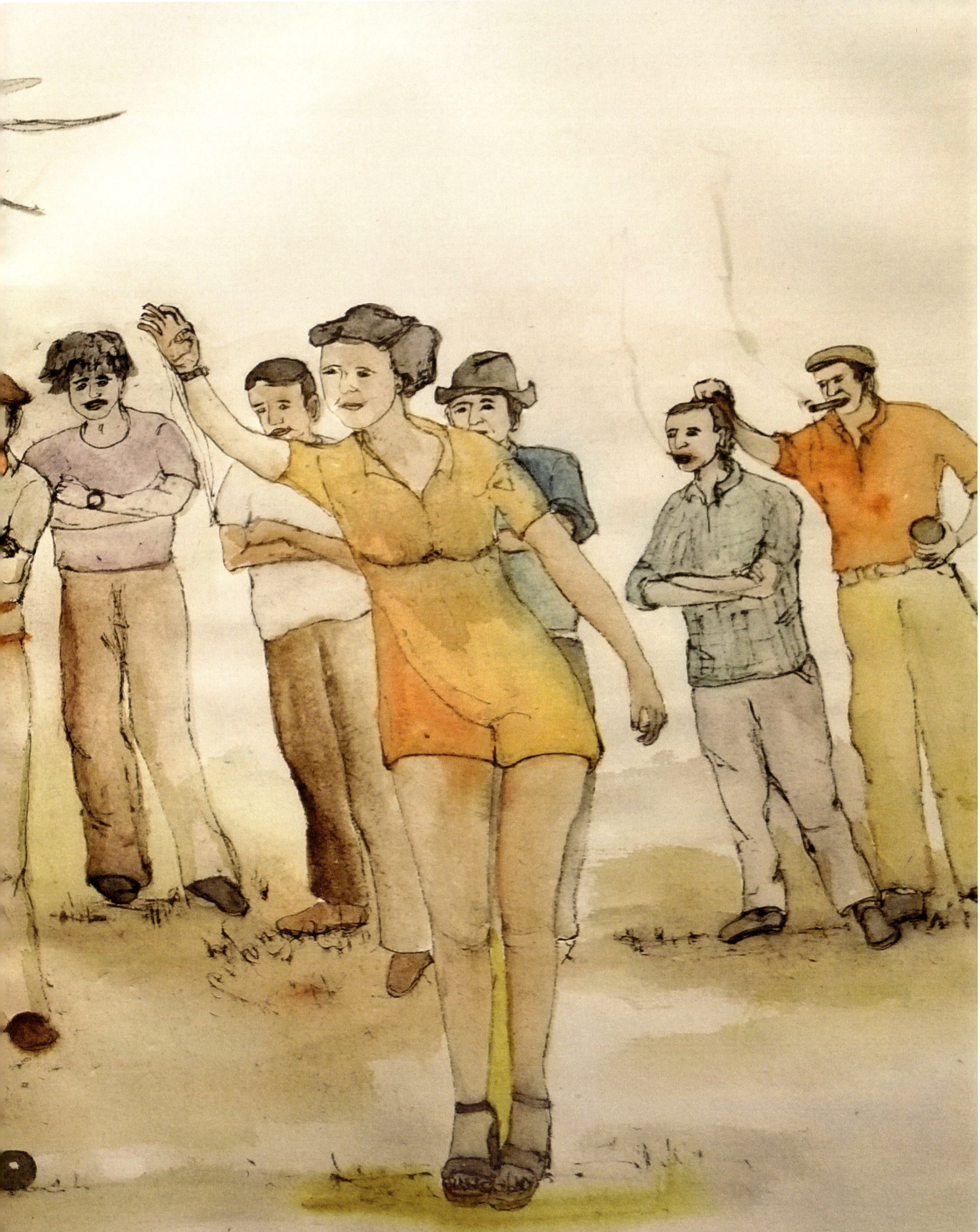

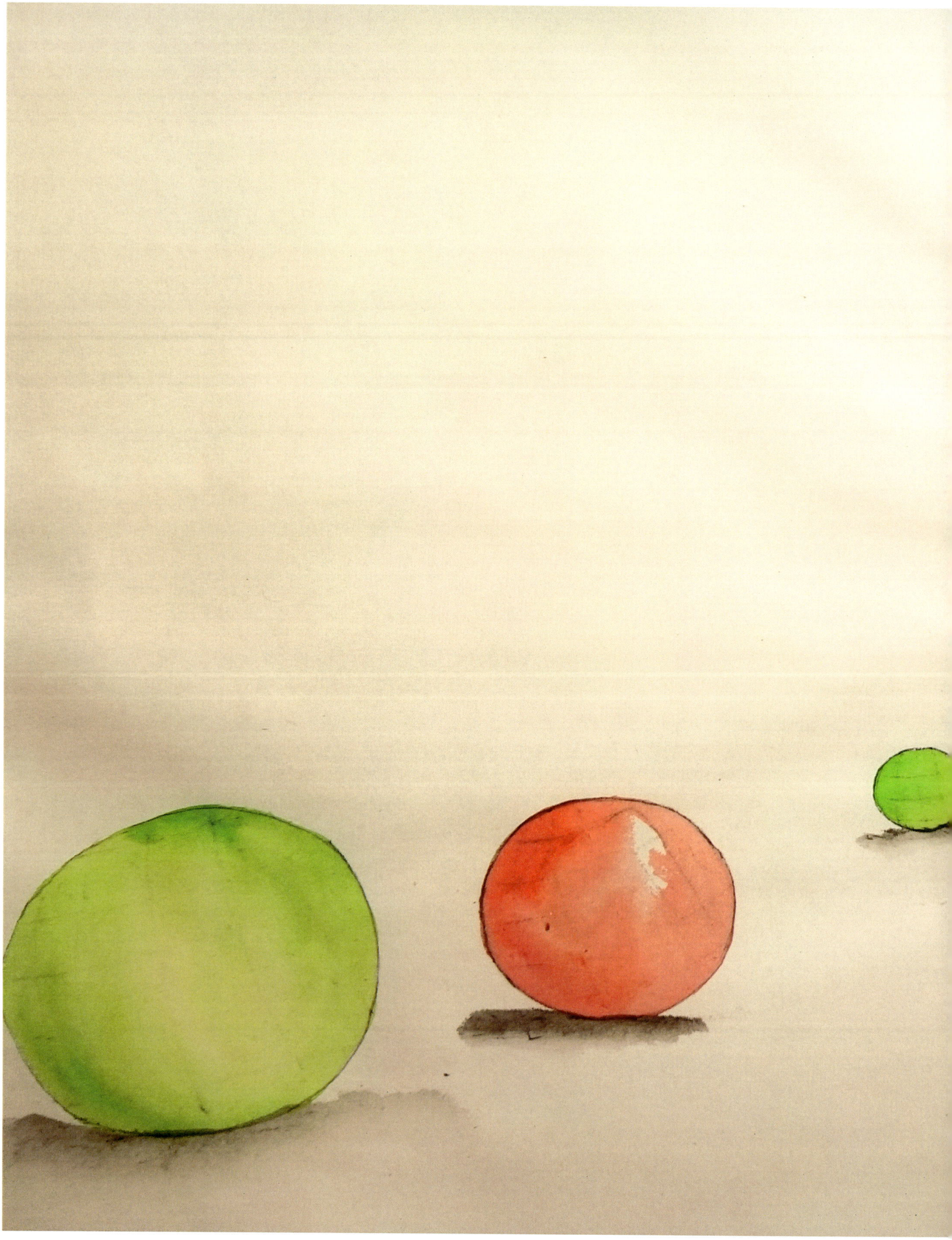

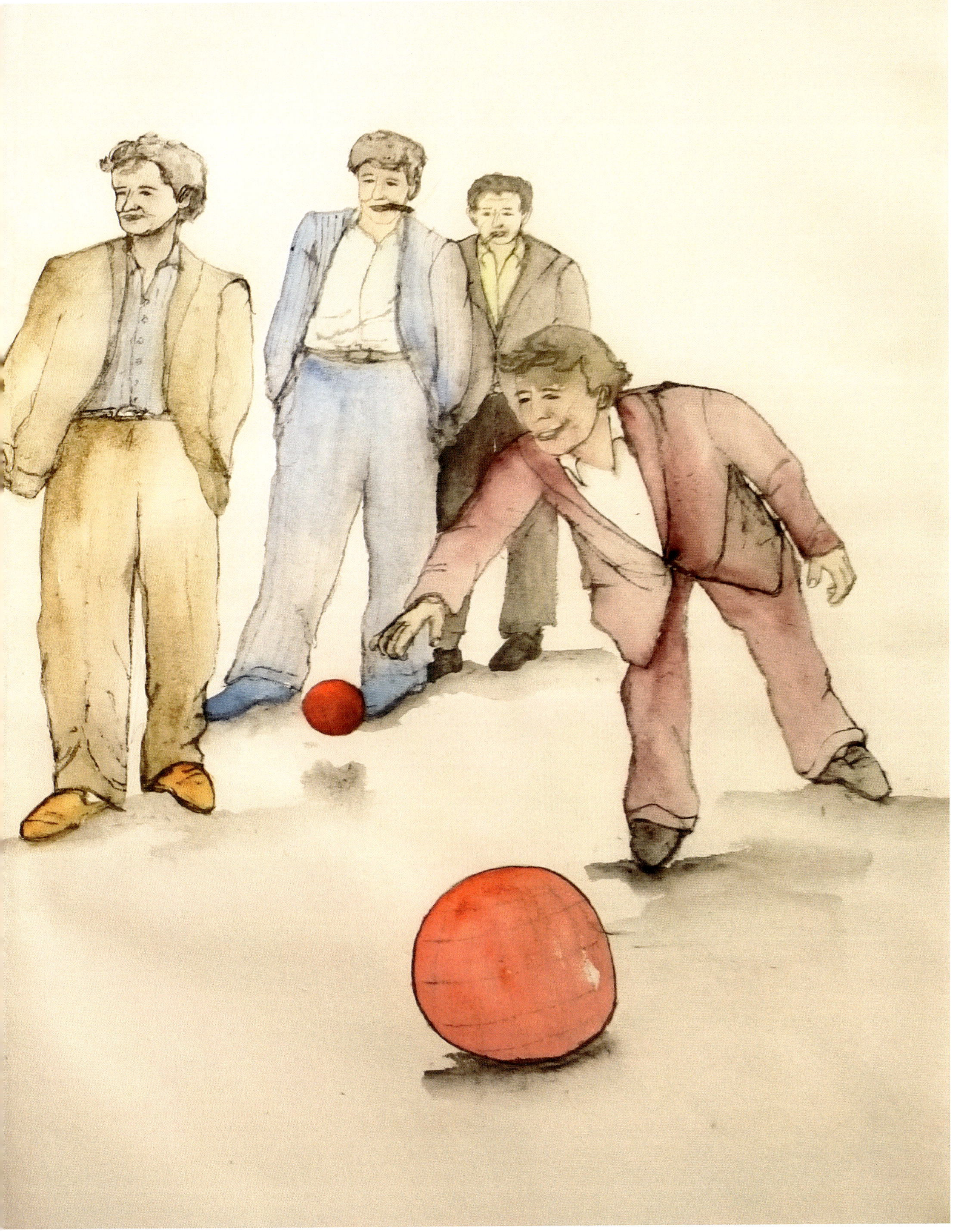

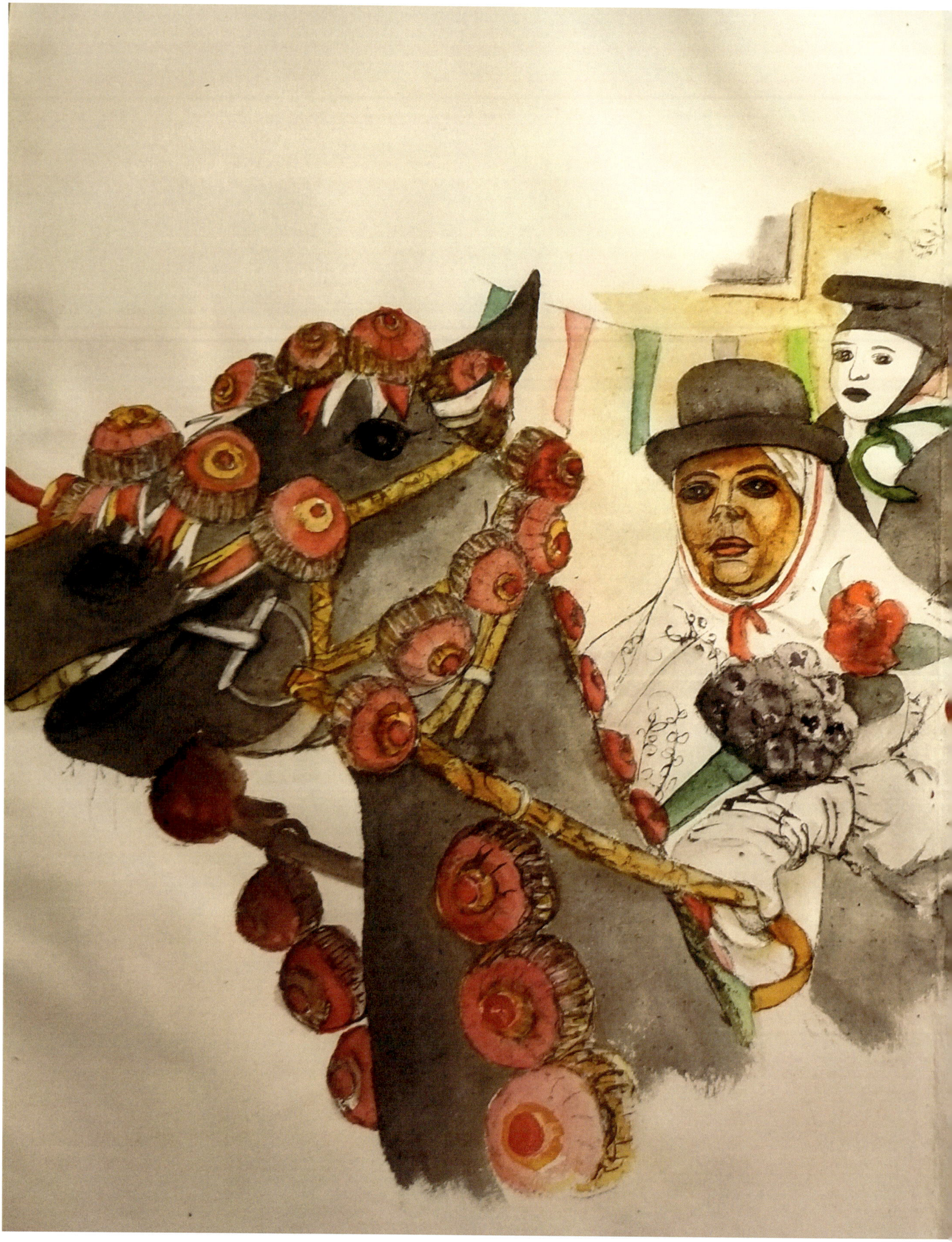

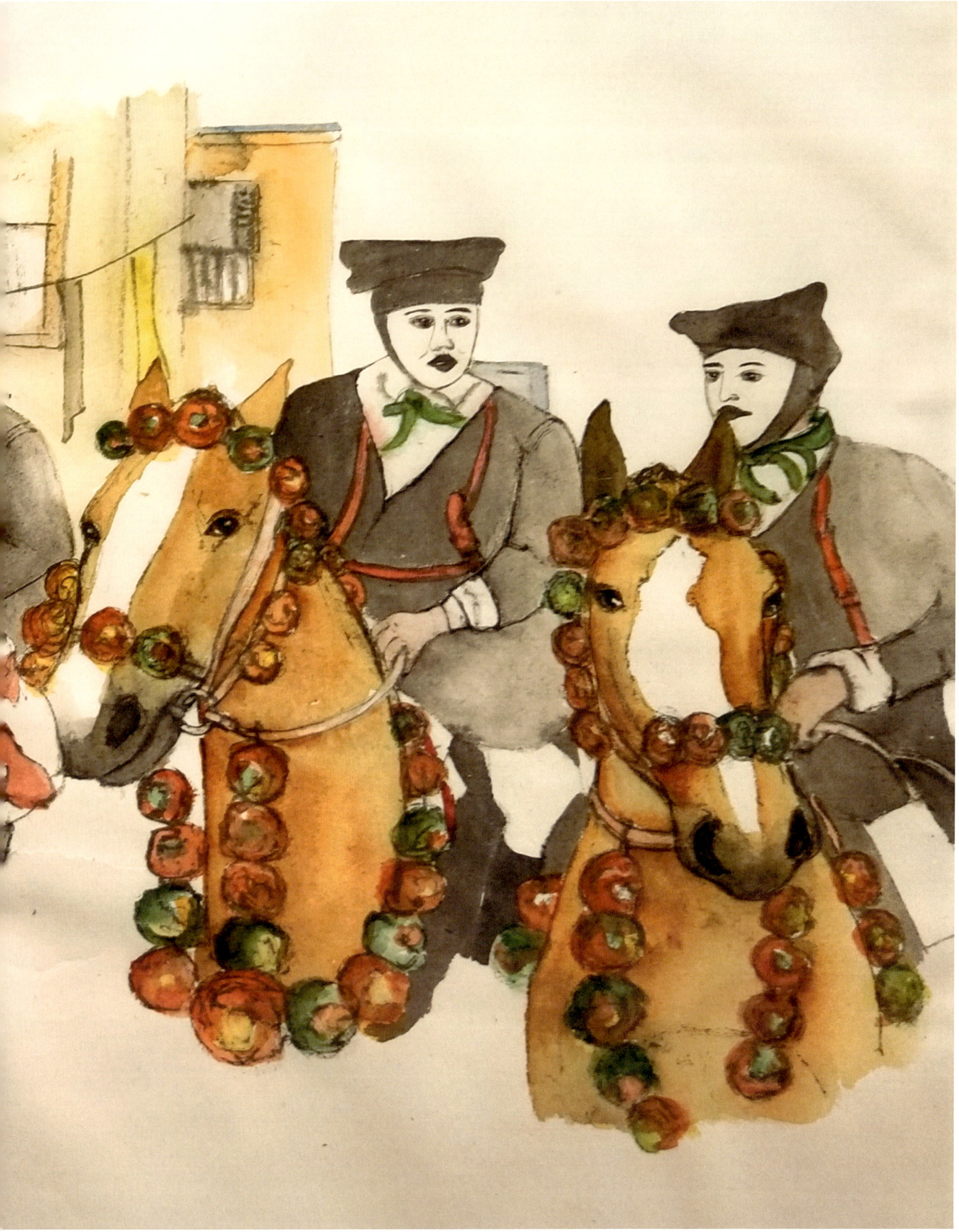

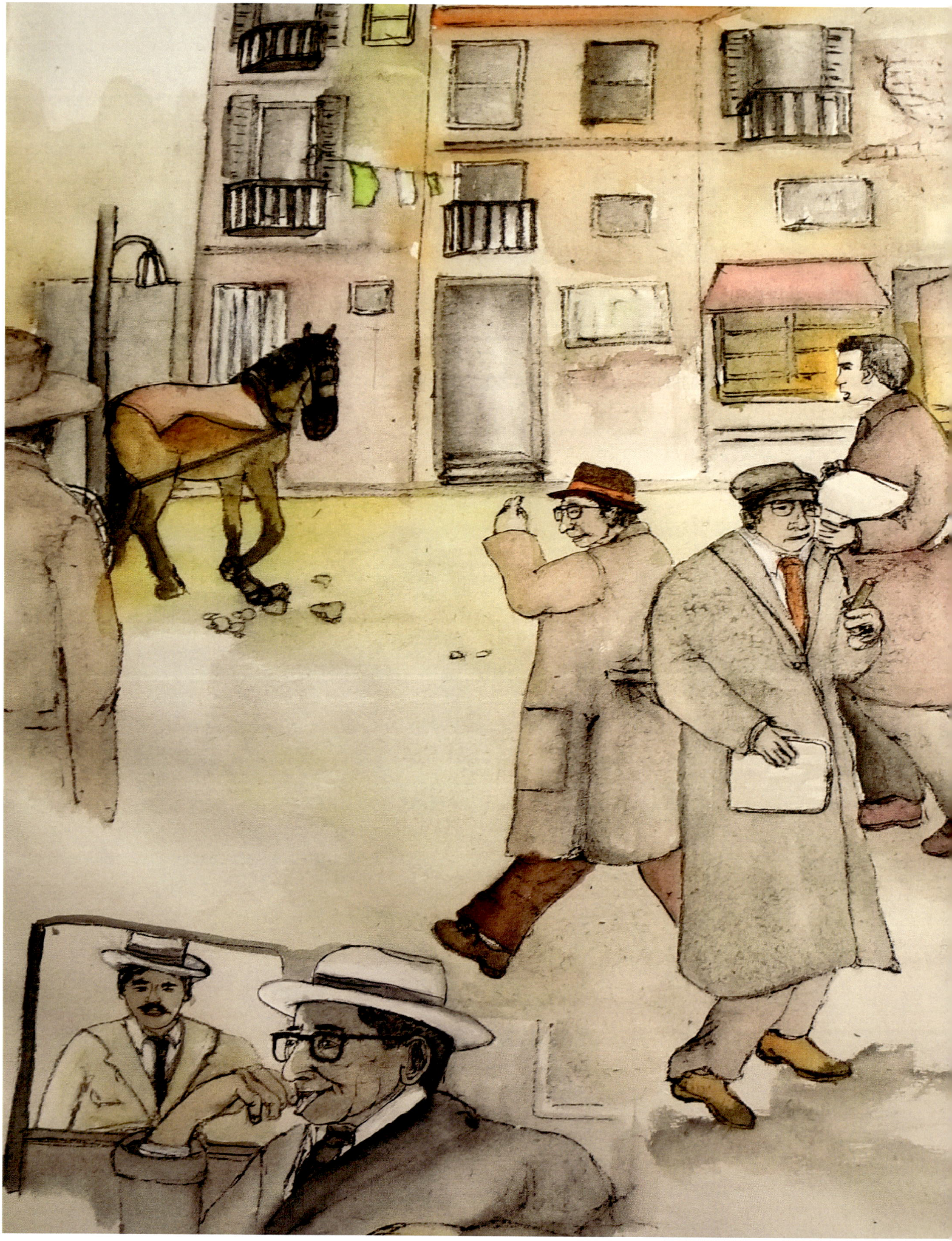

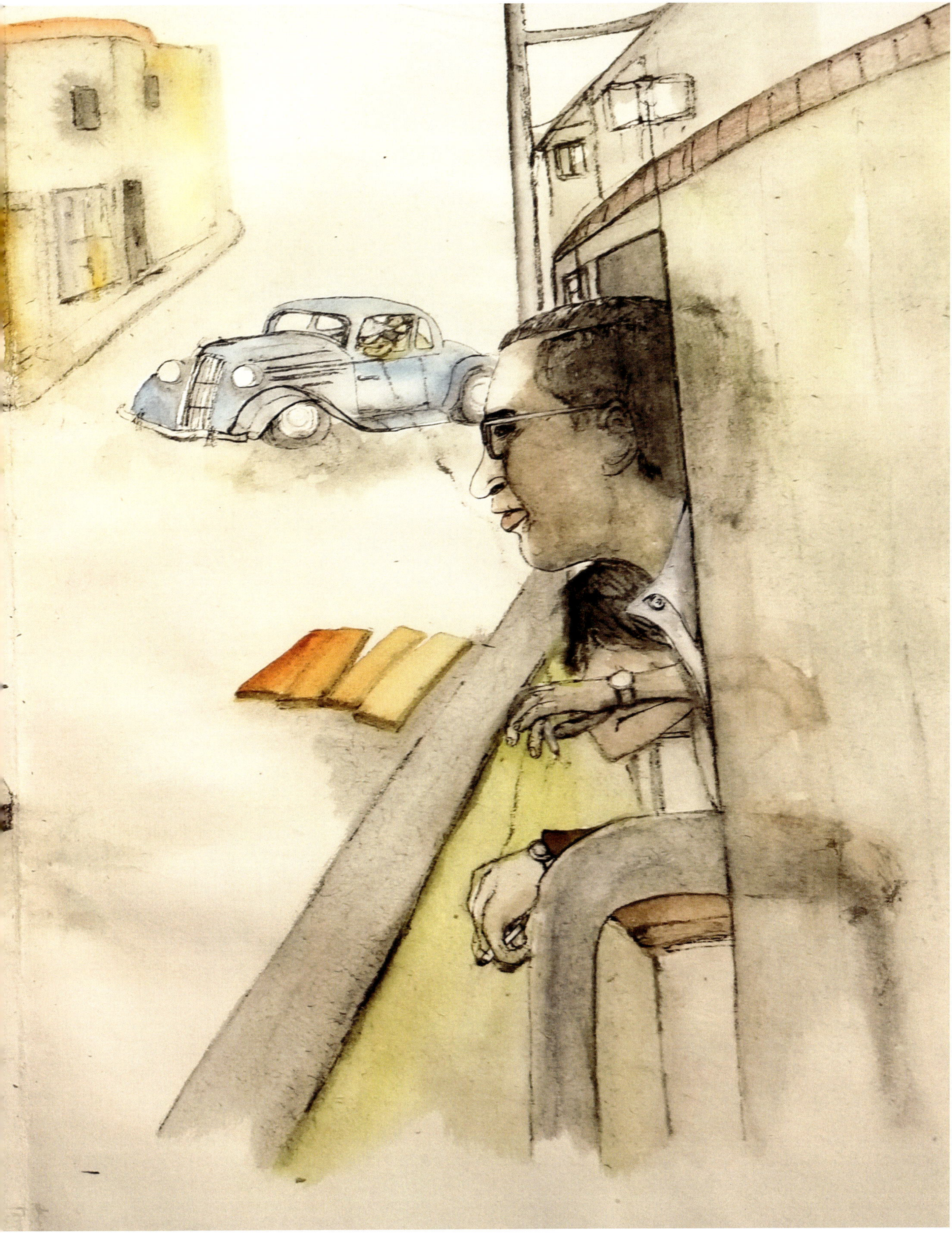

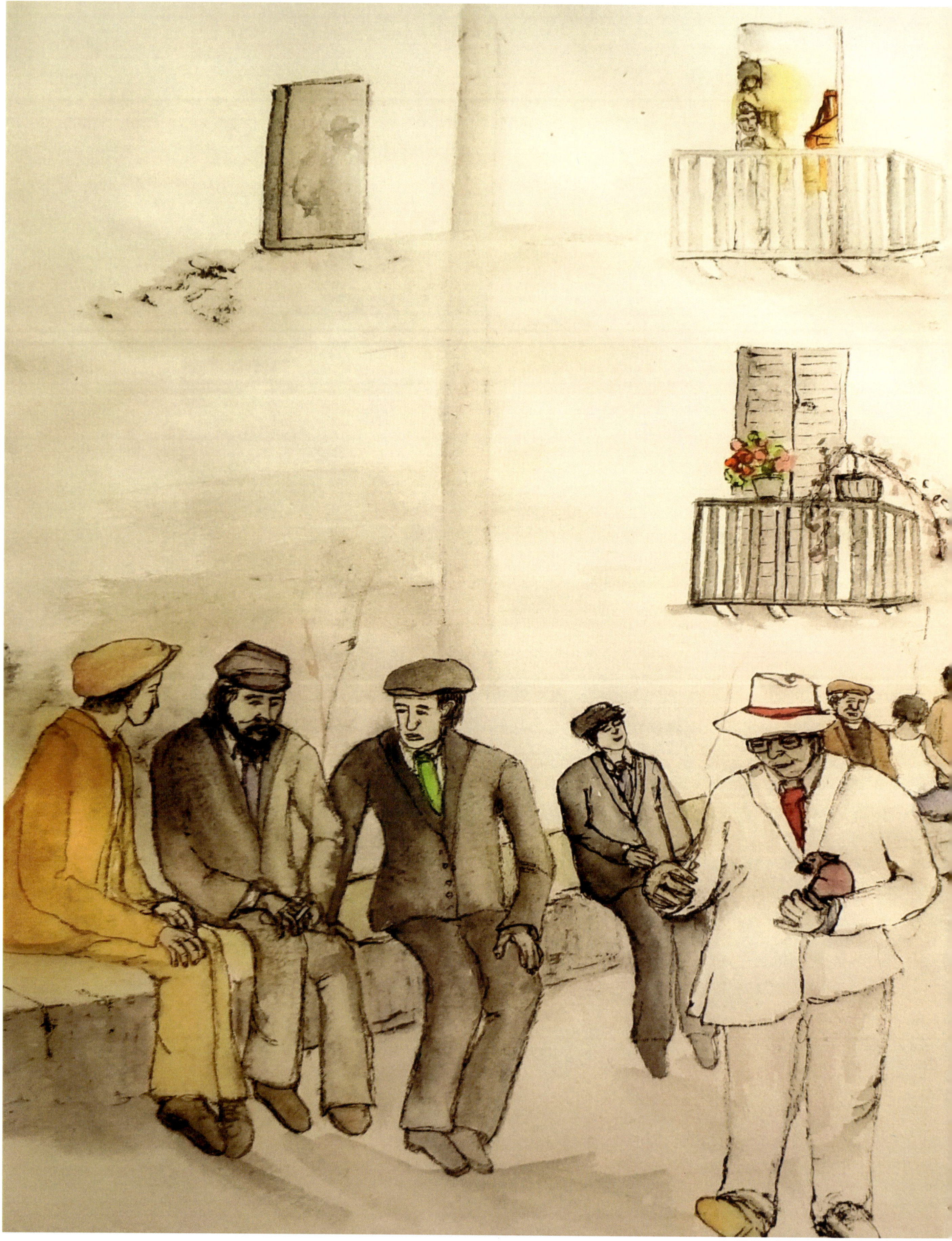

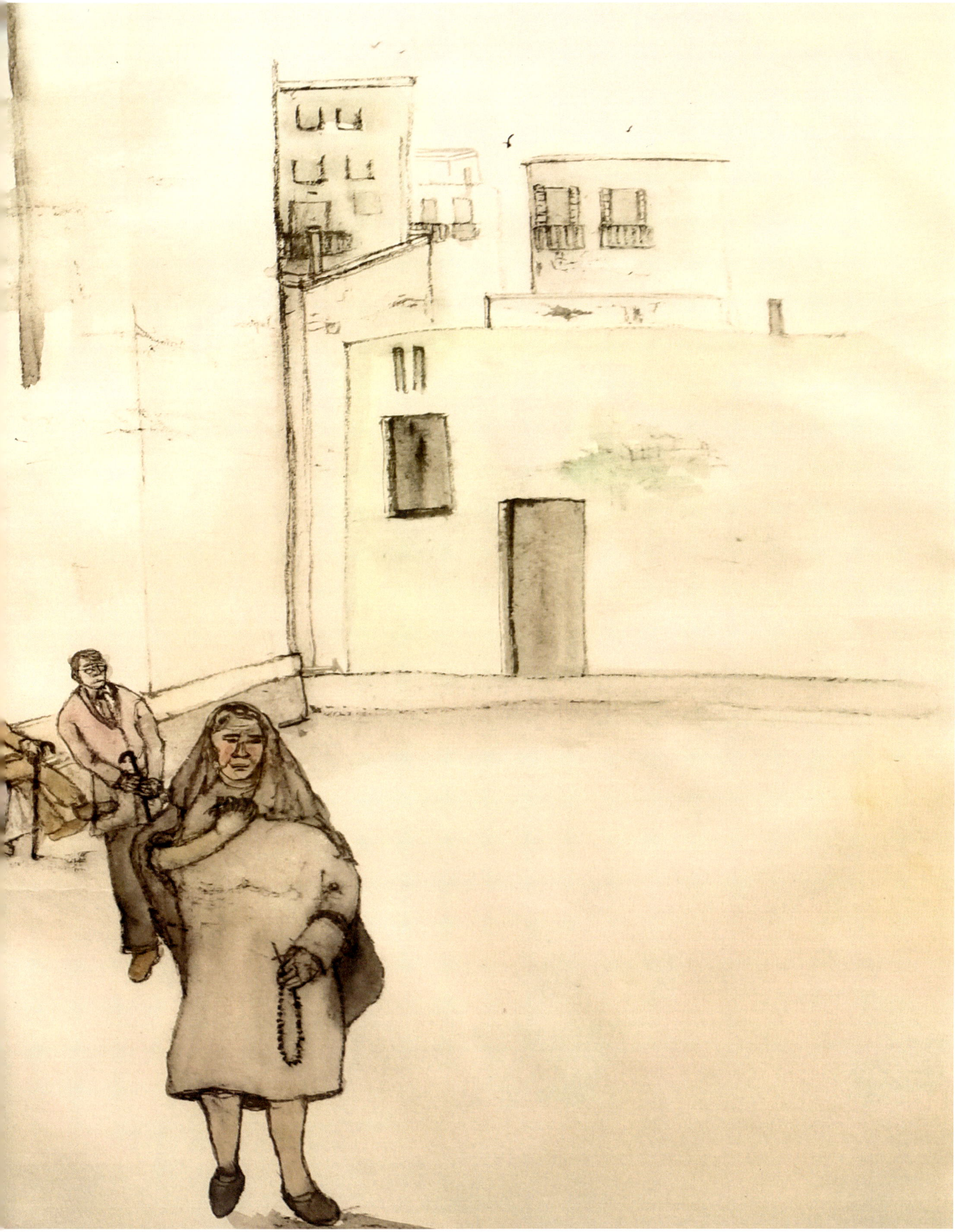

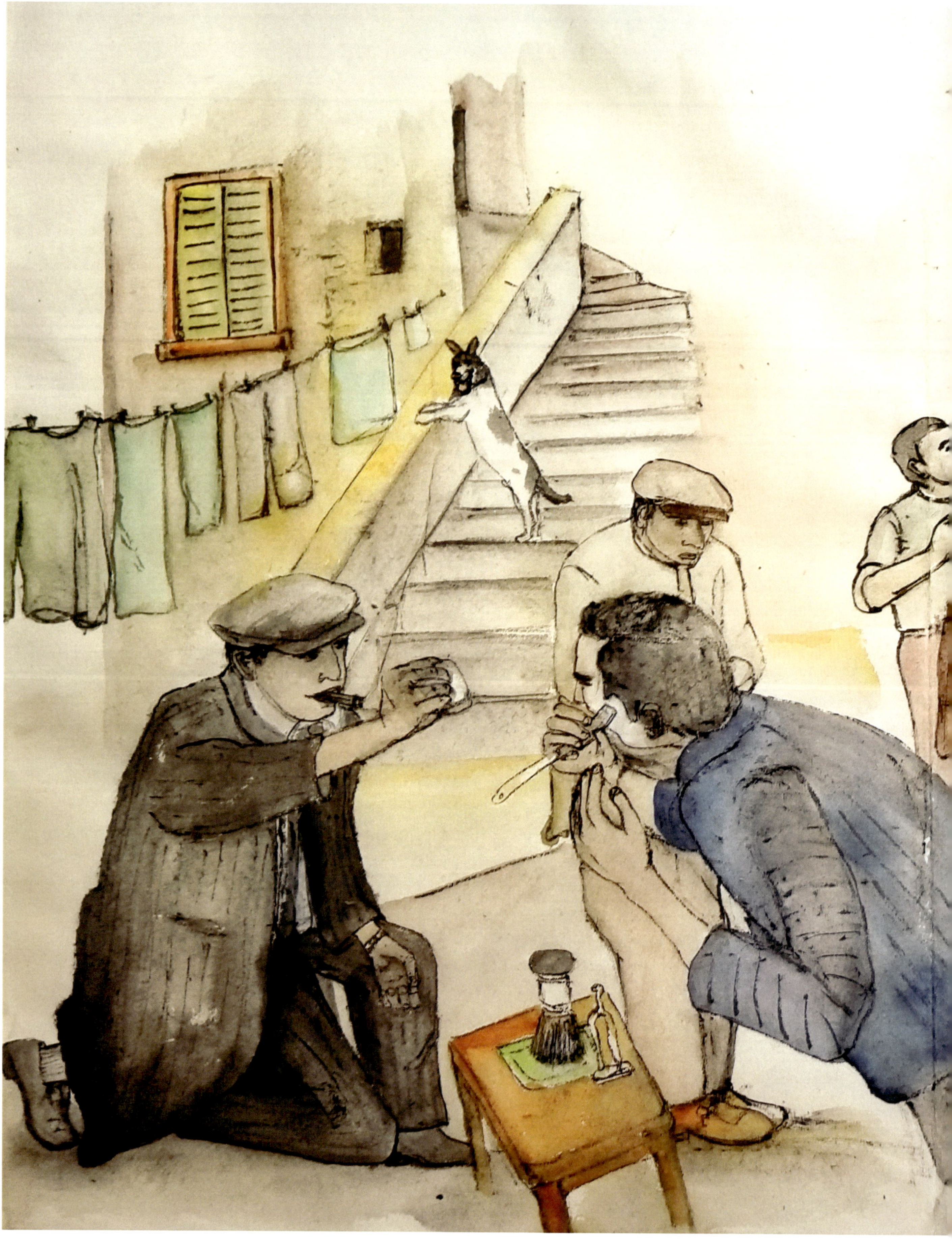

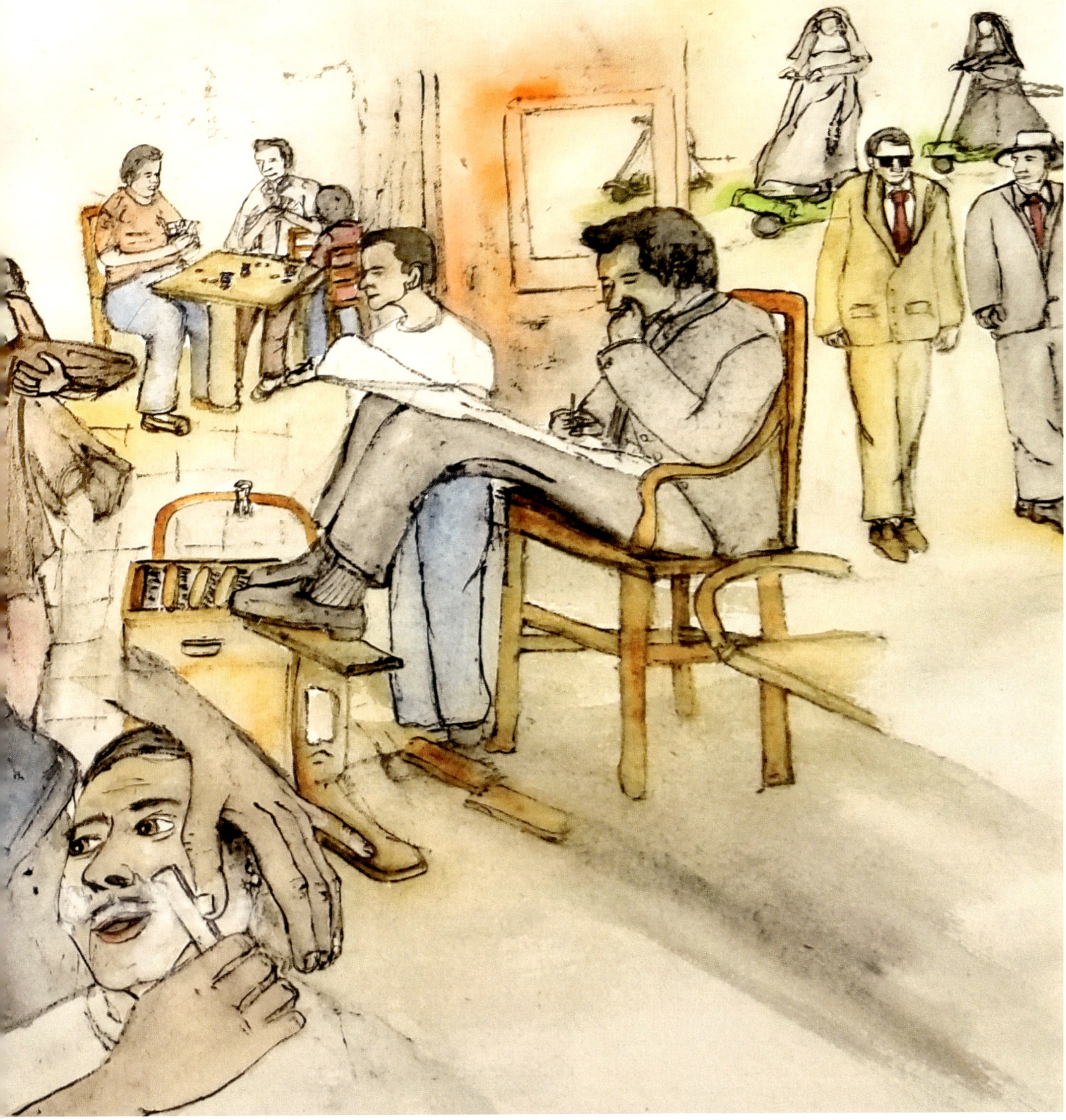

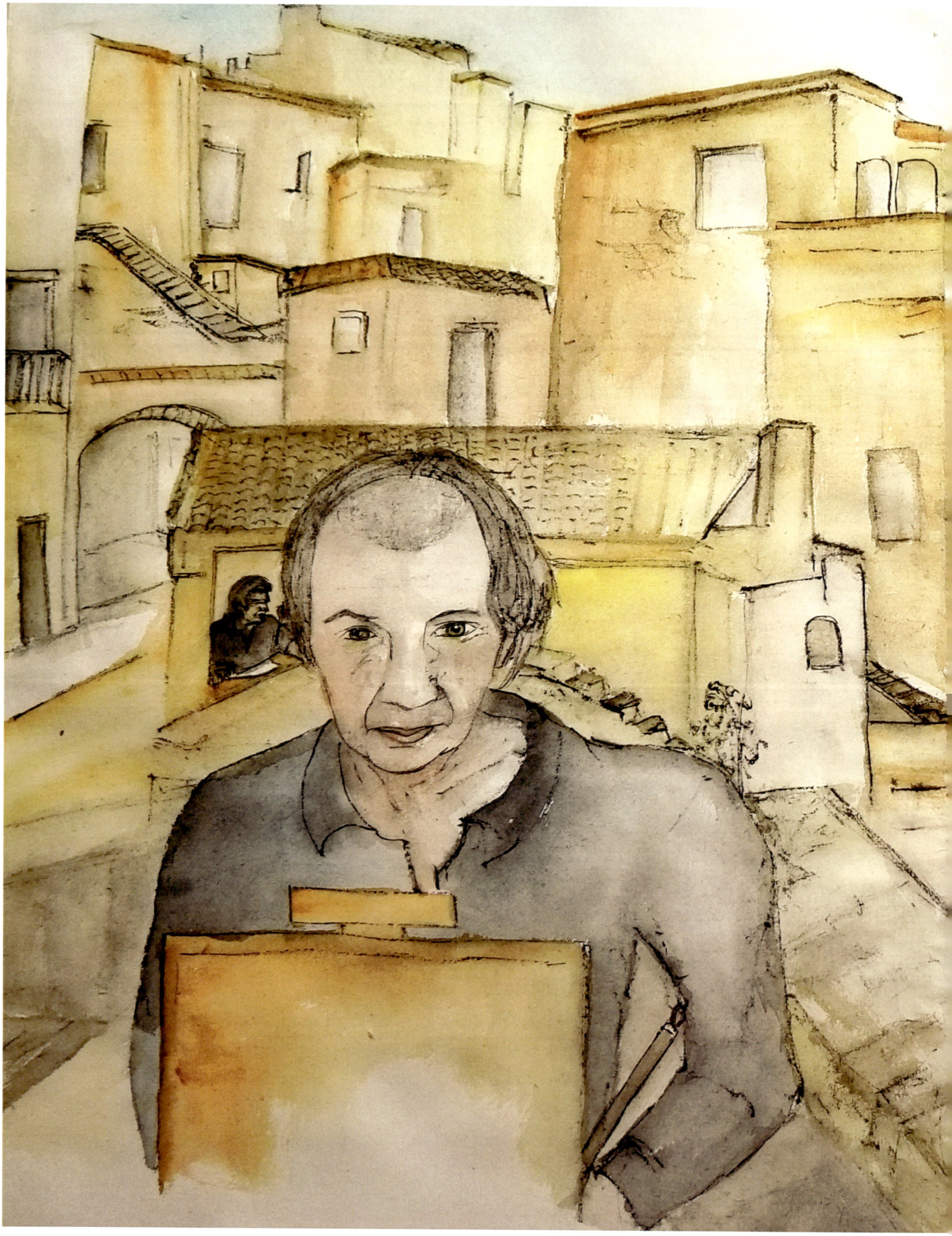

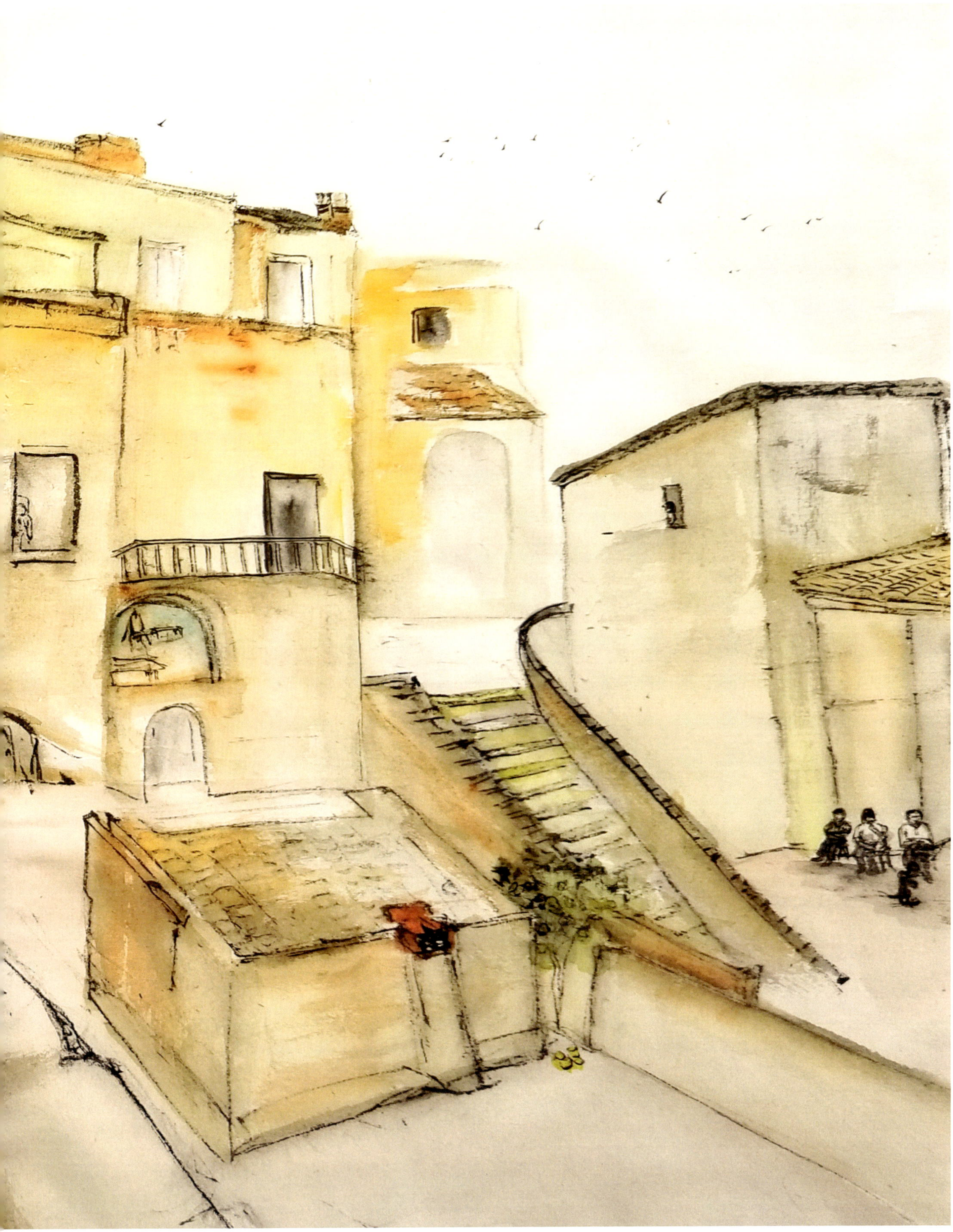

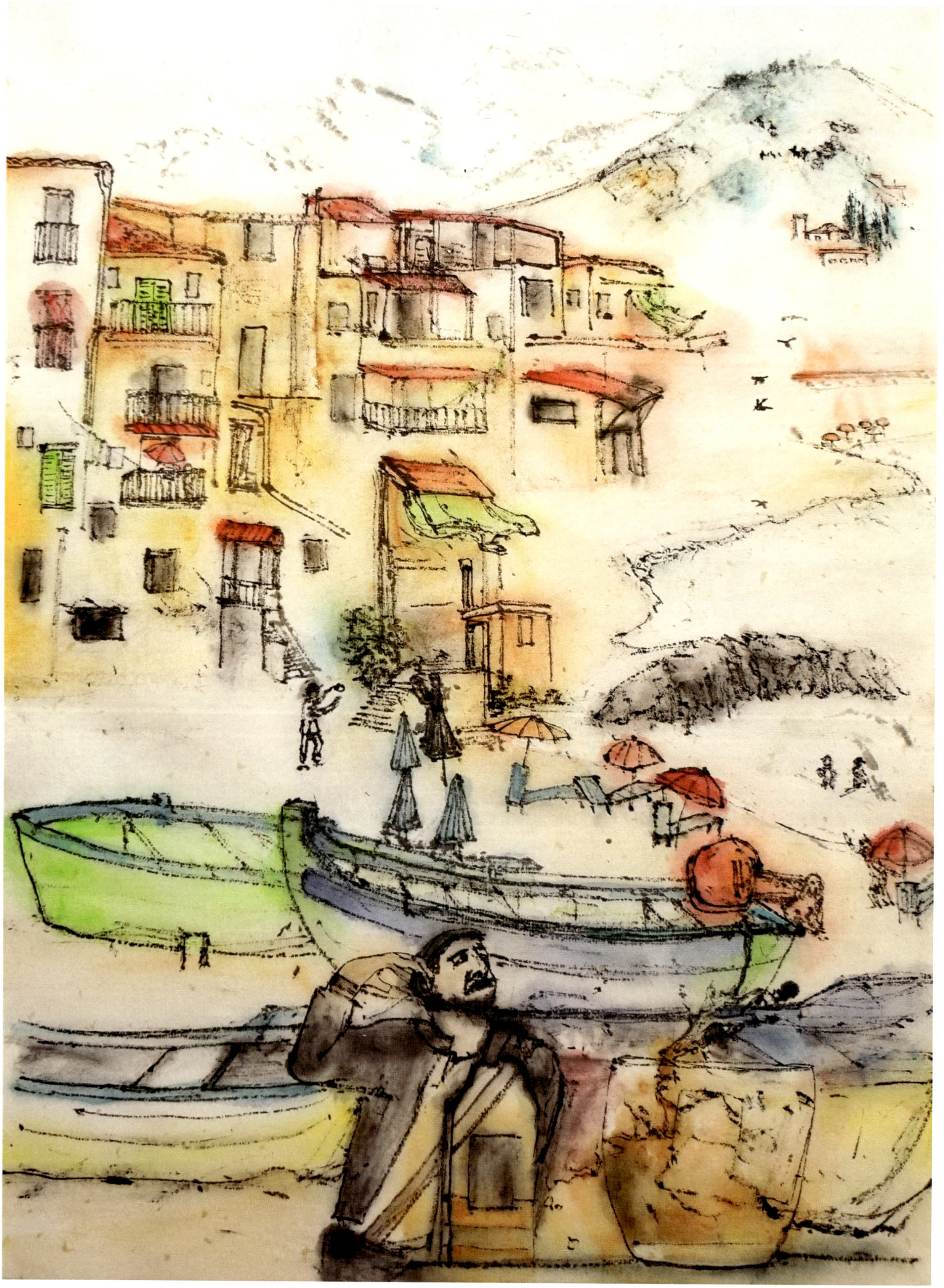

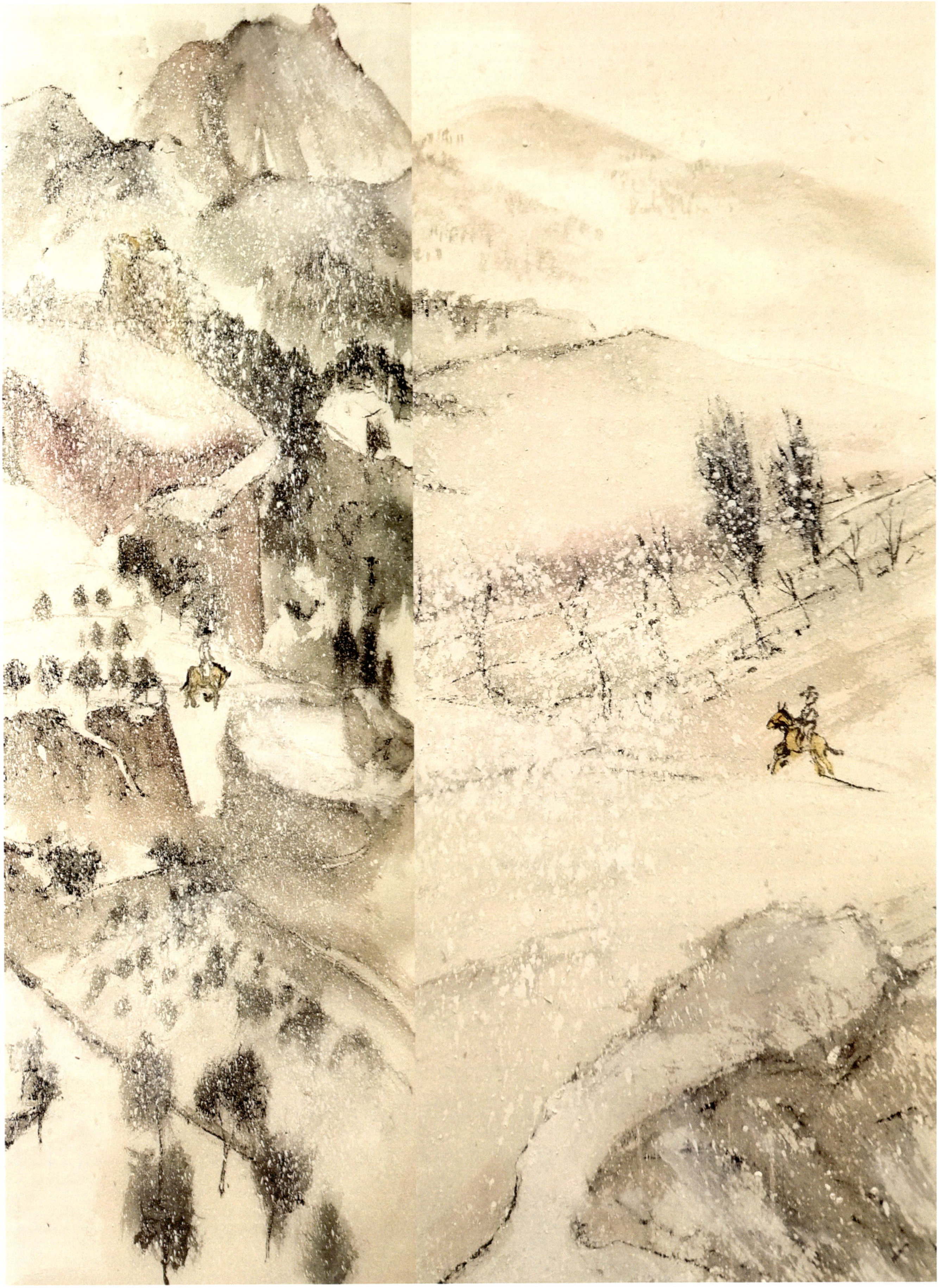

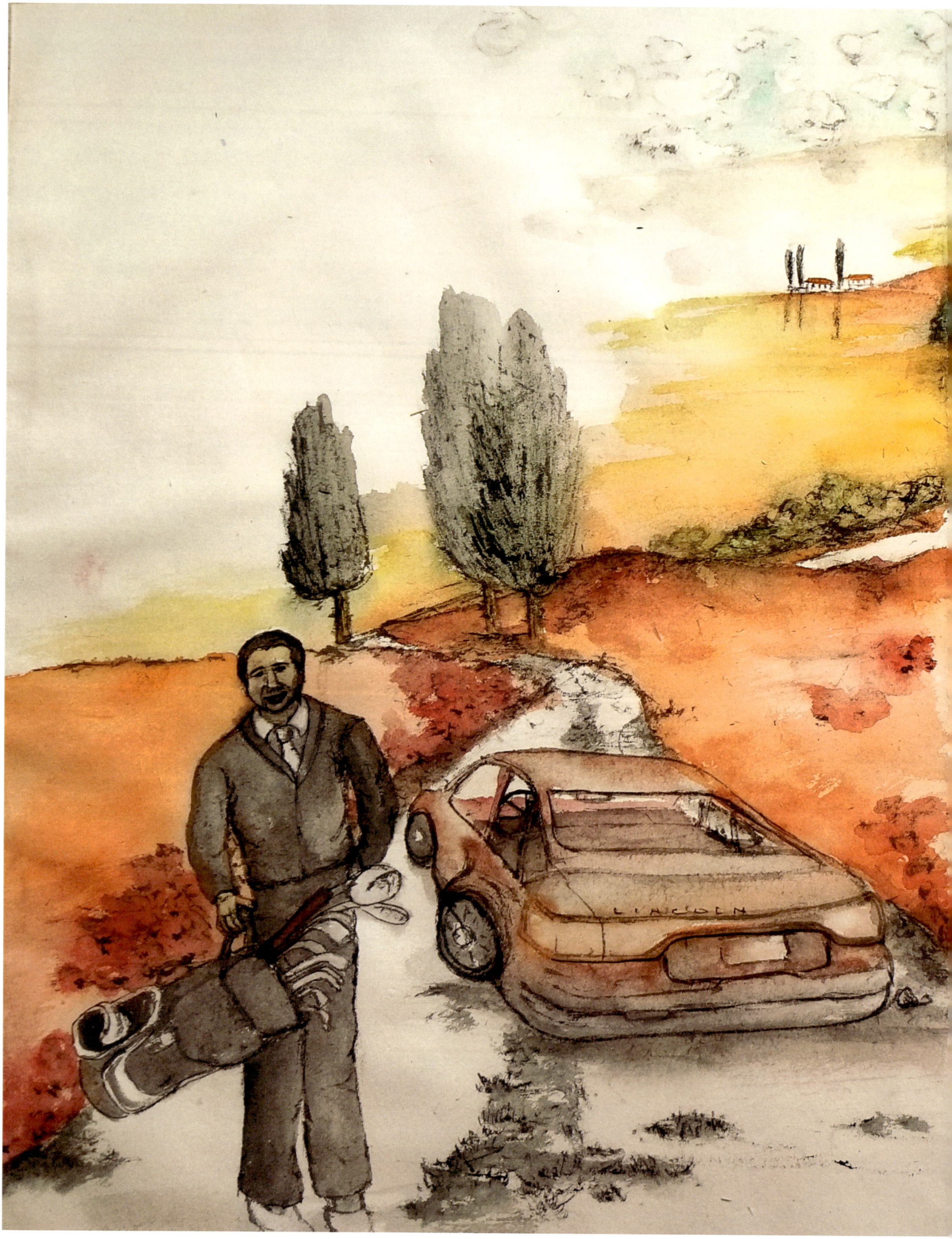
LINCOLN

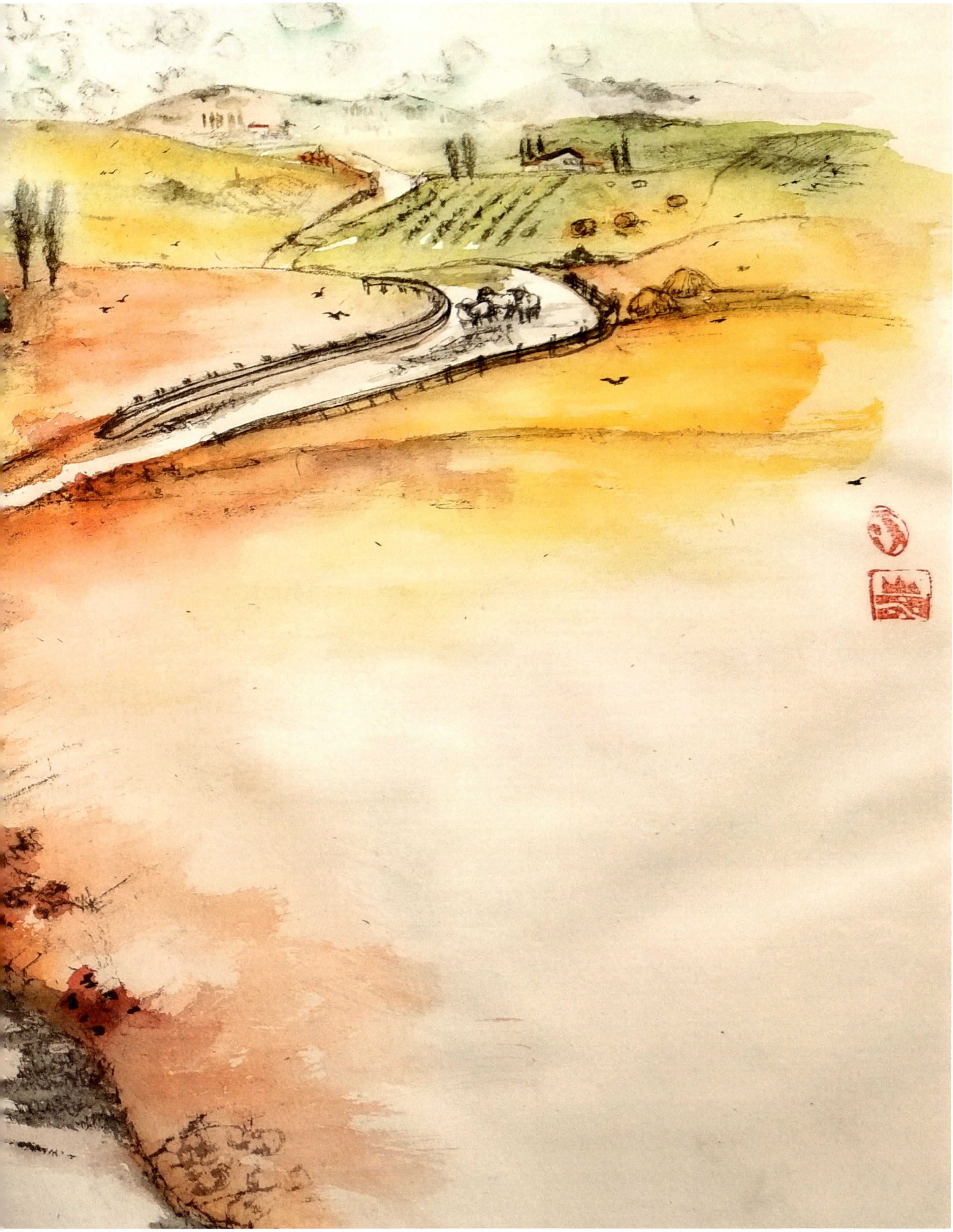

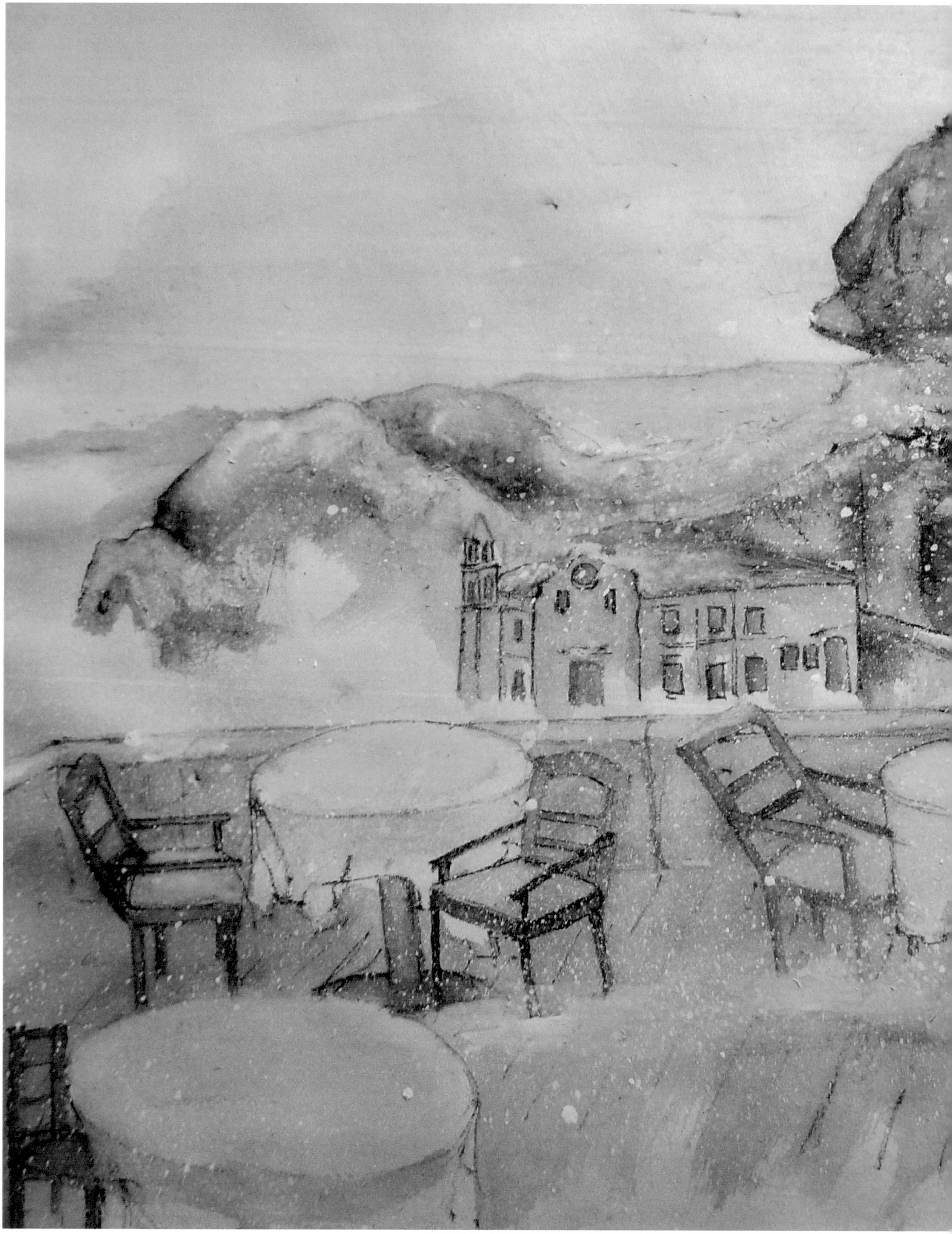

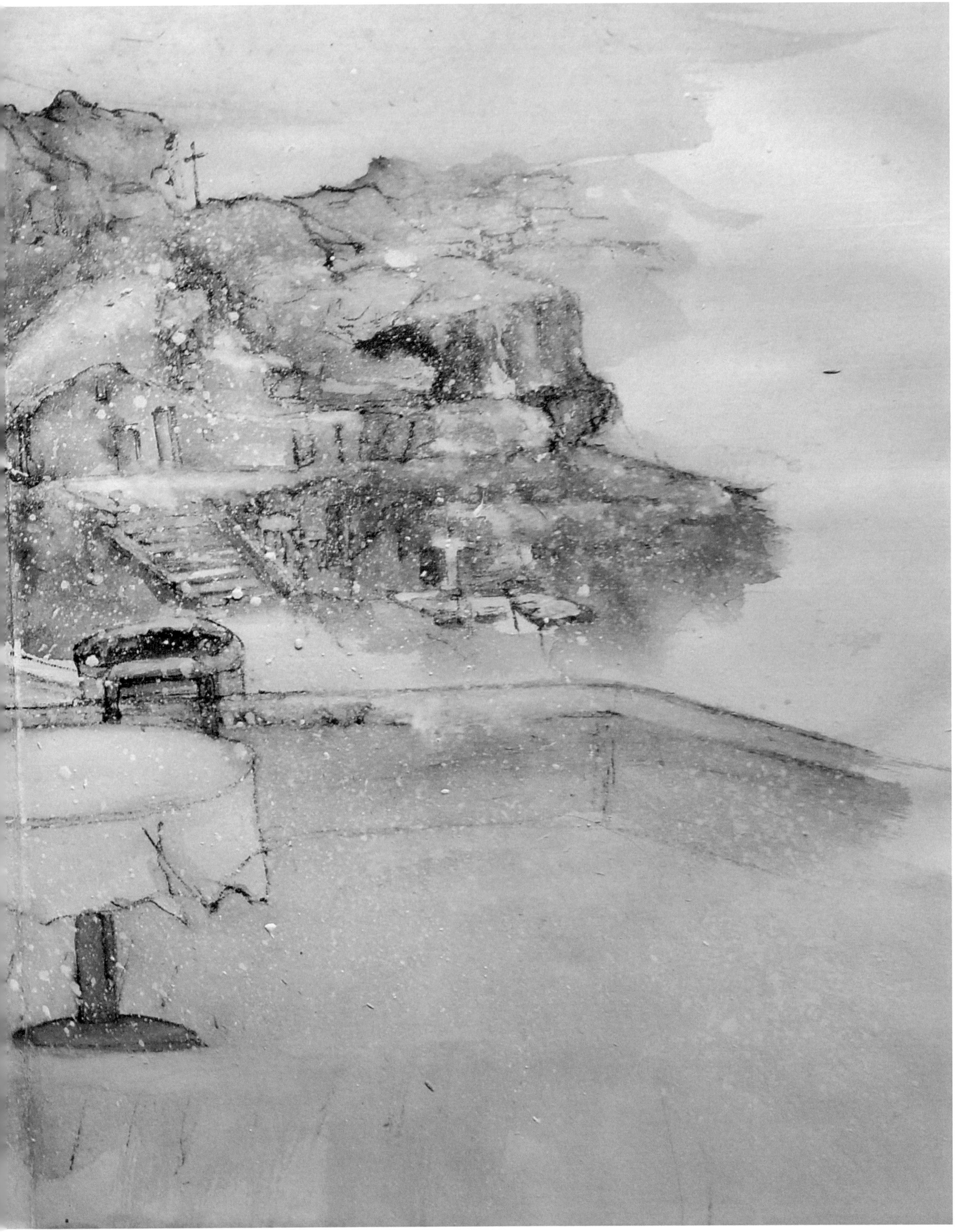

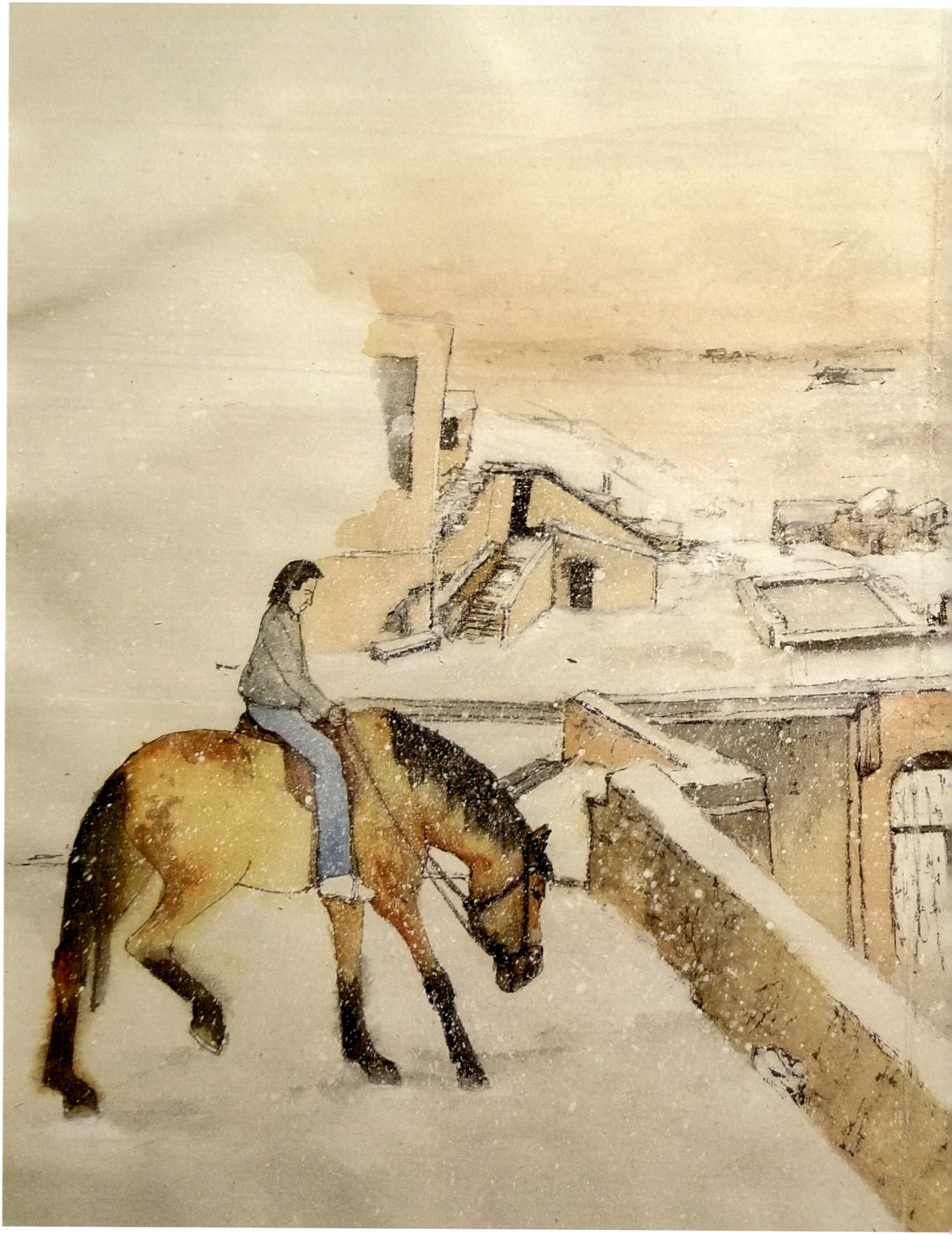

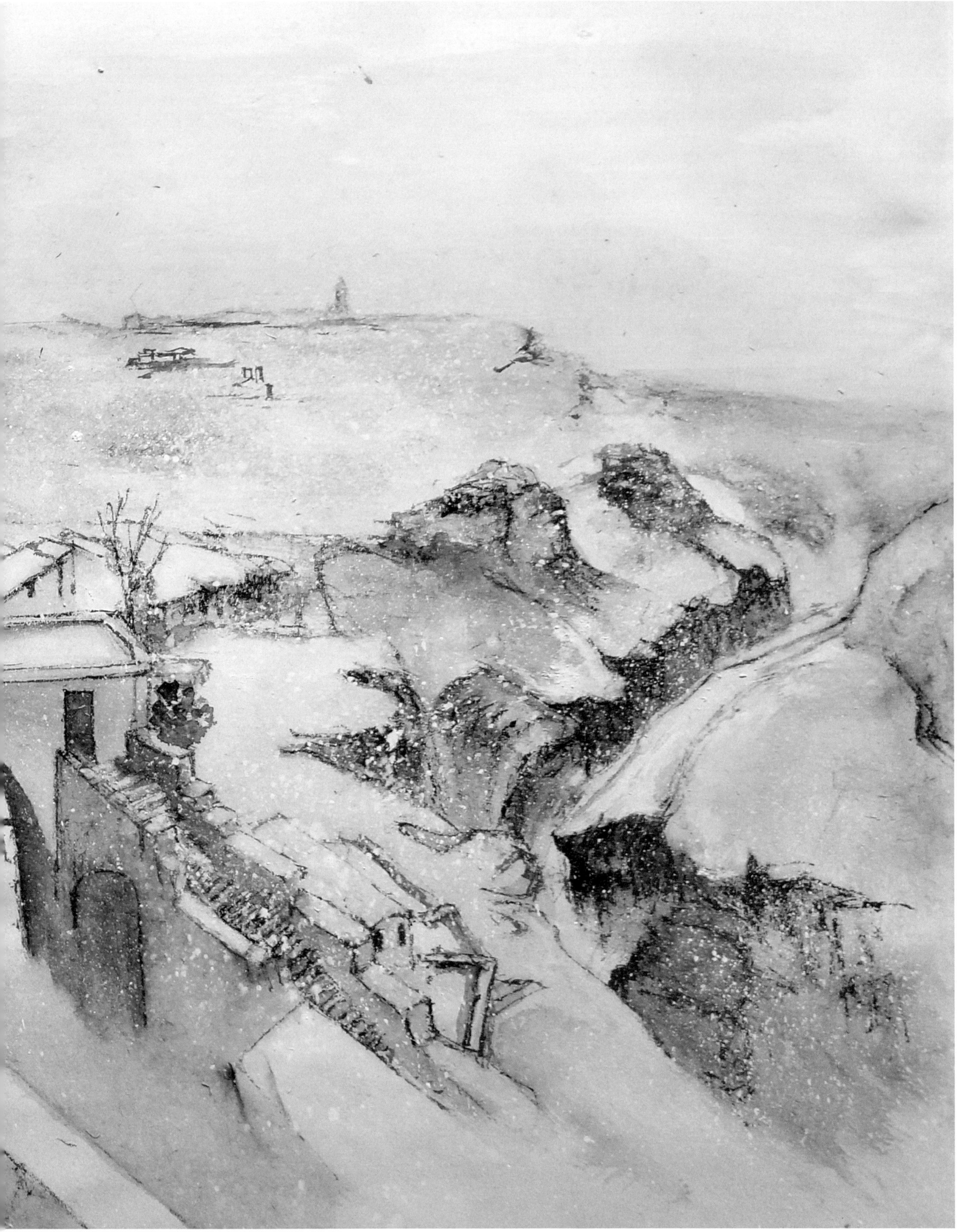

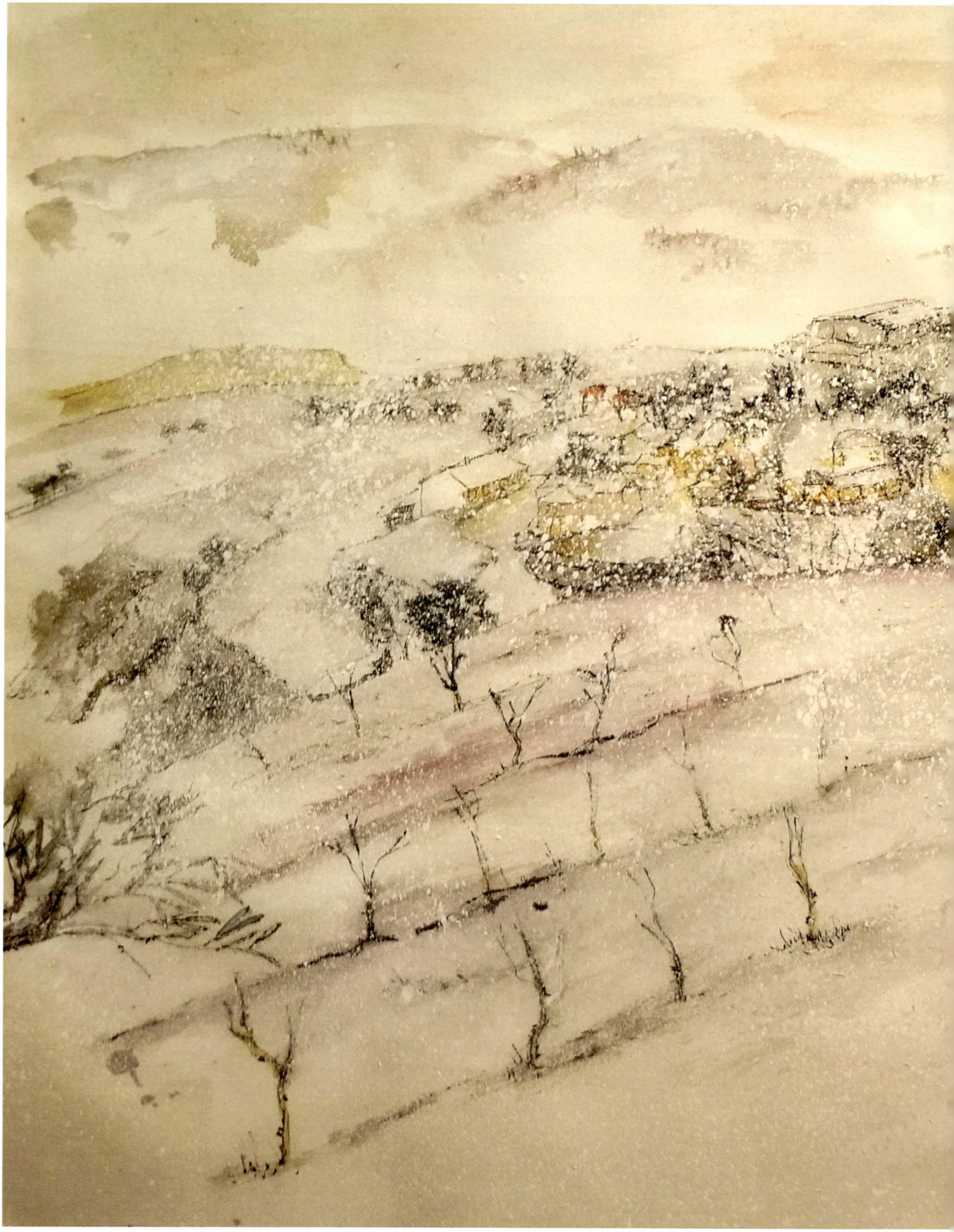

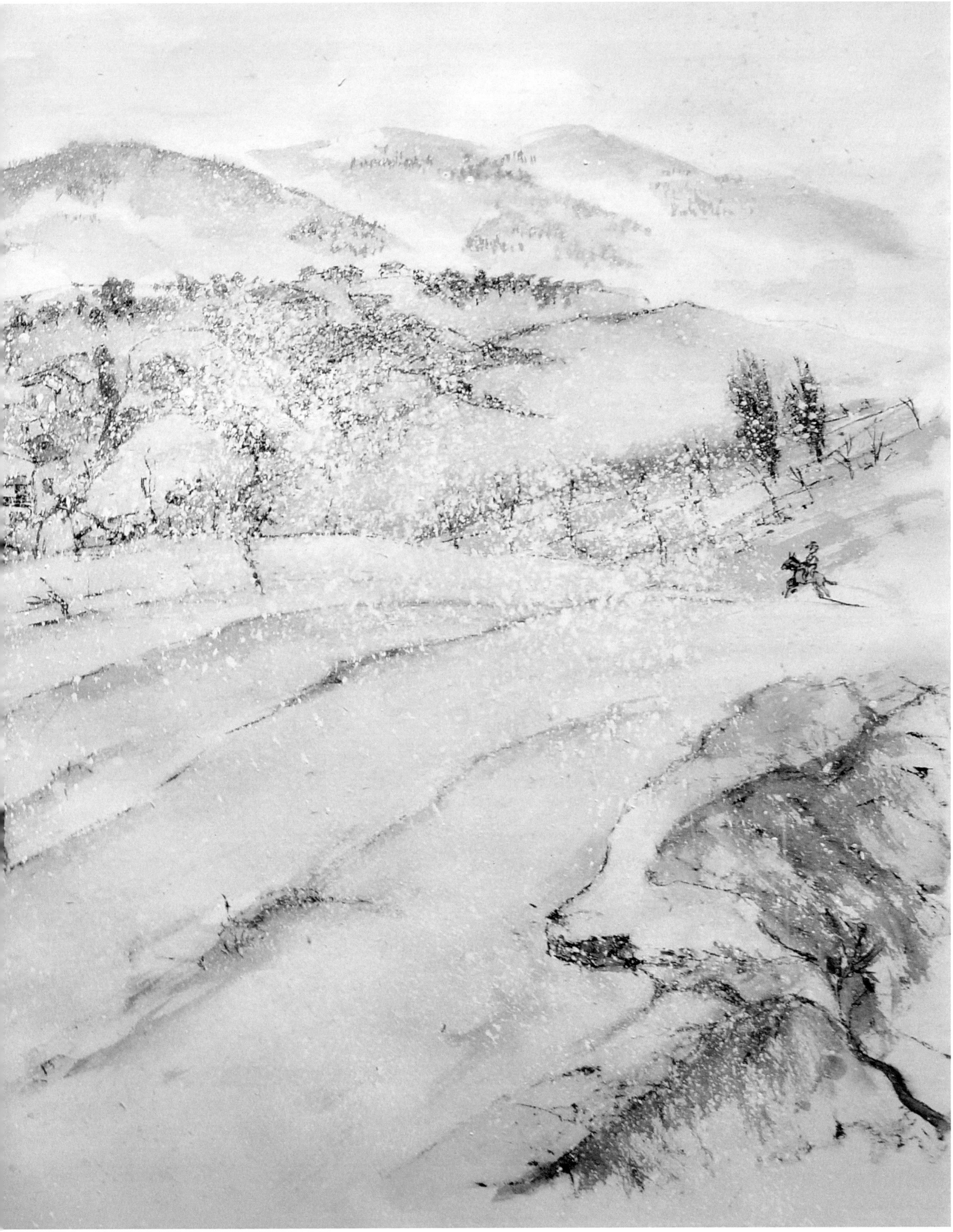

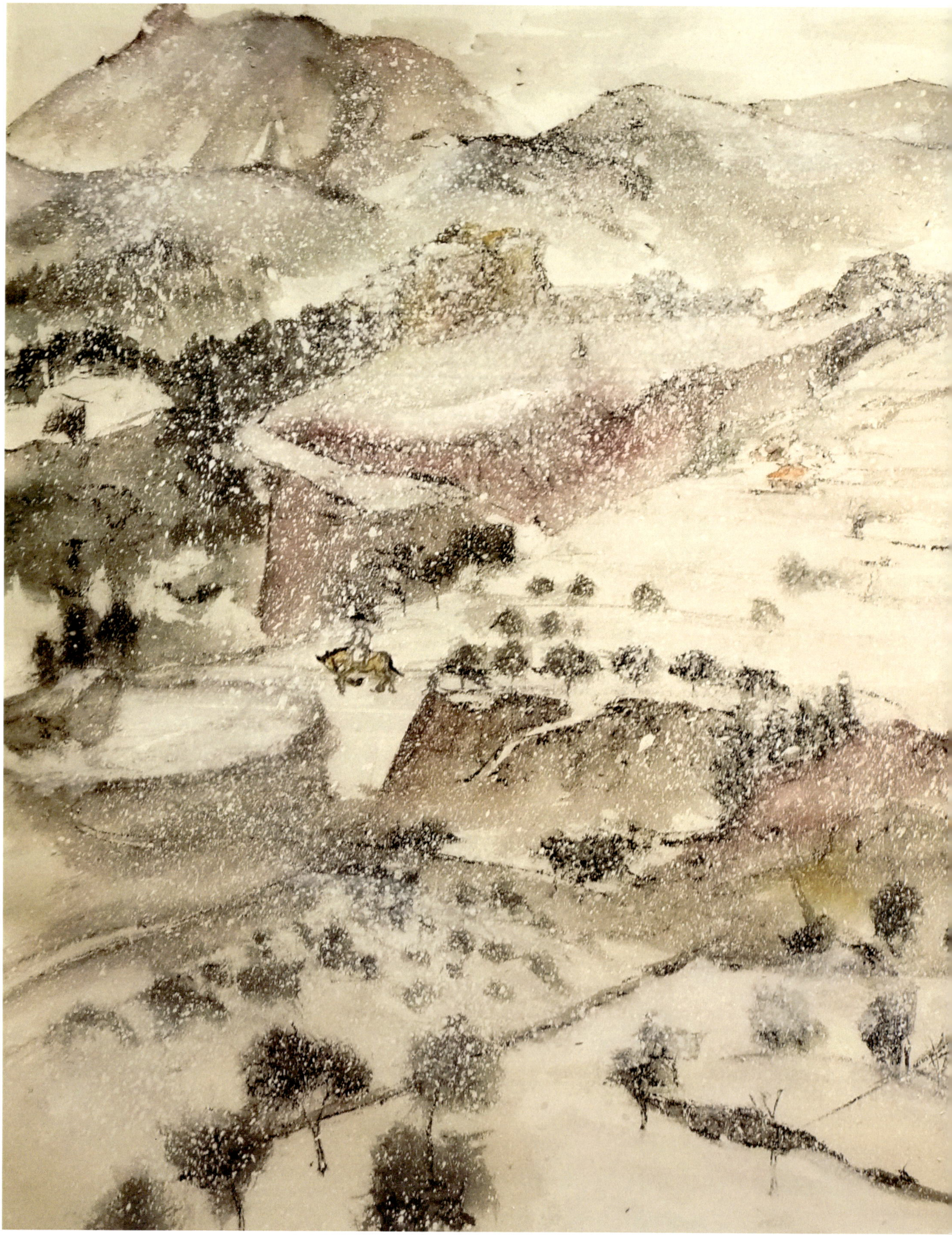

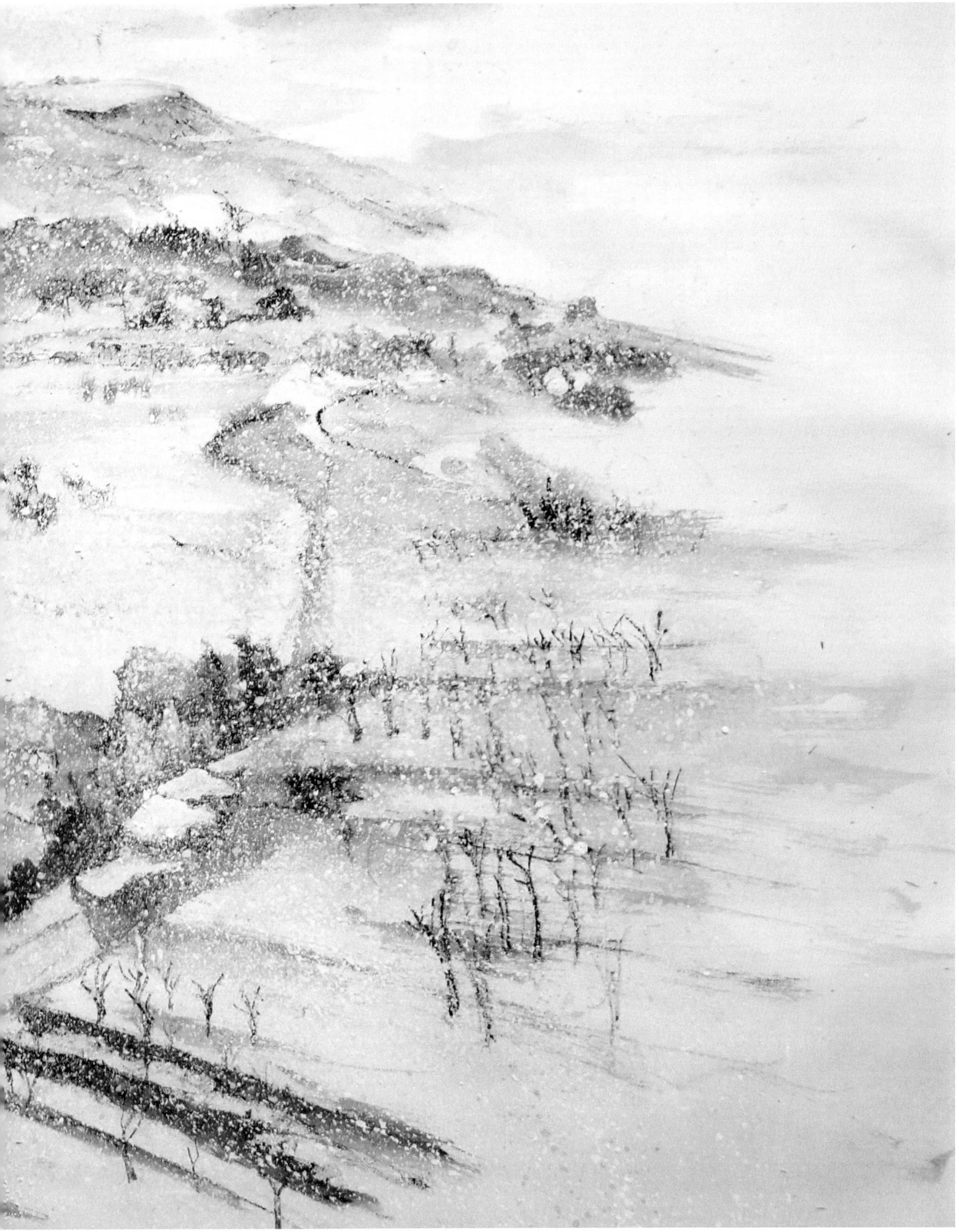

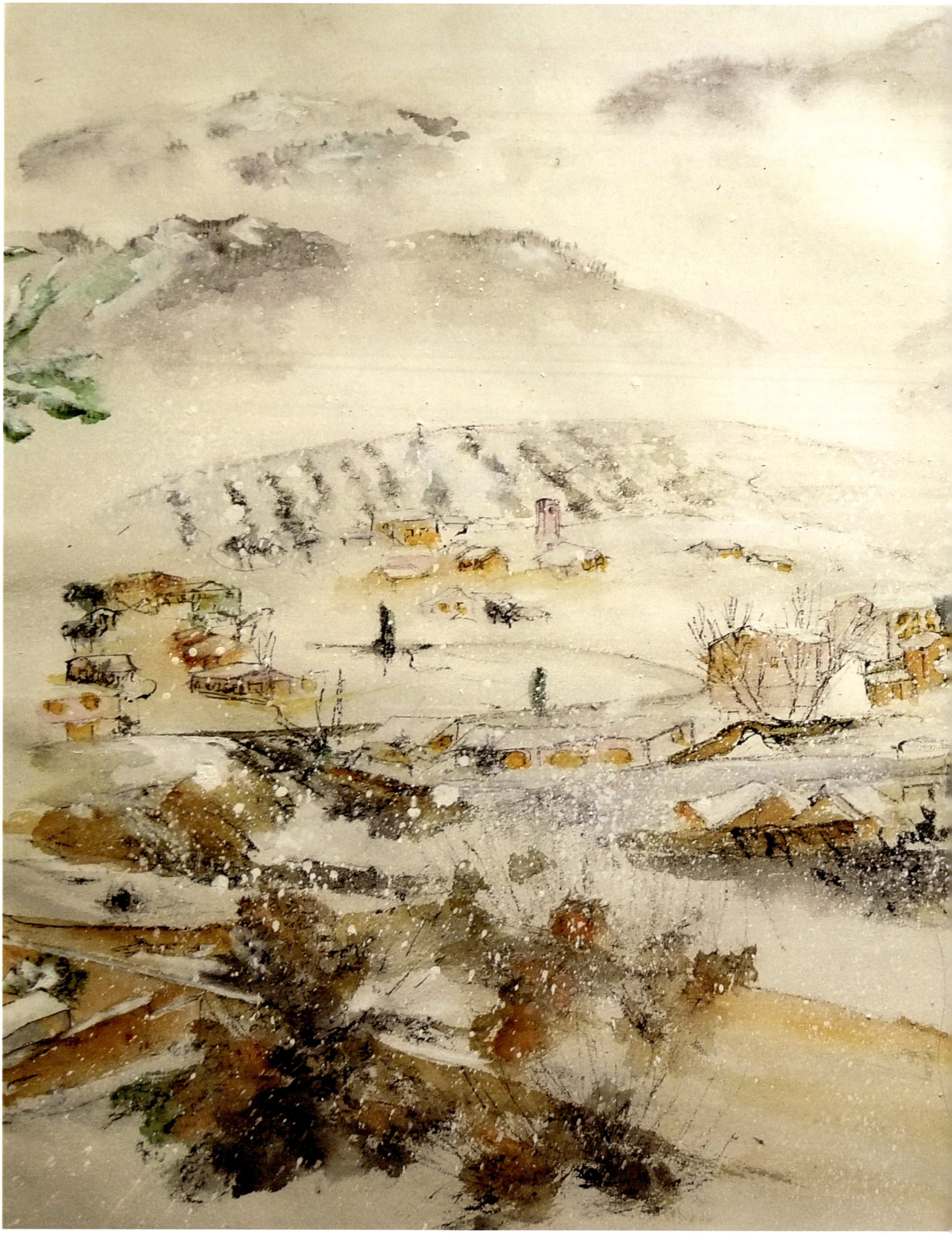

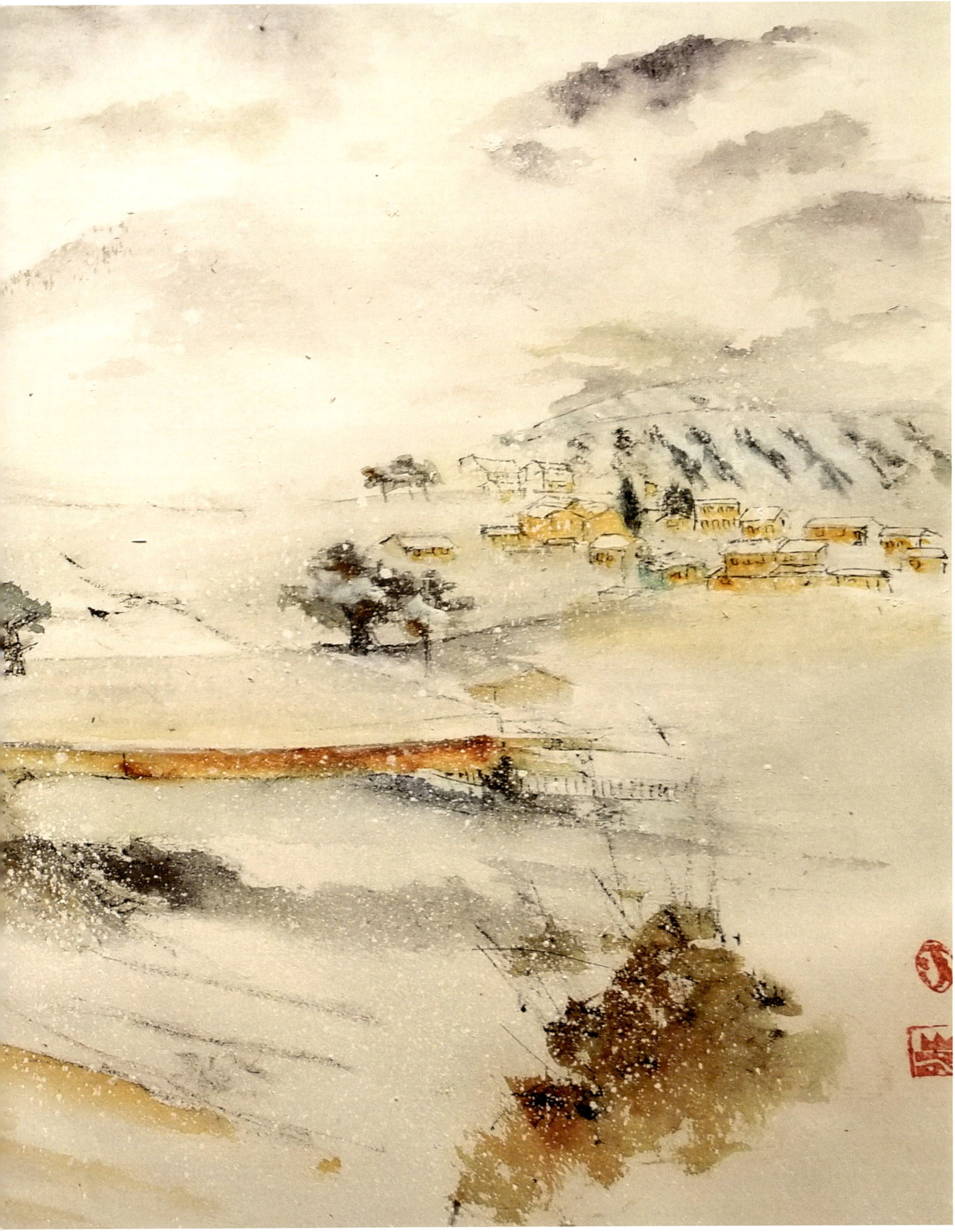

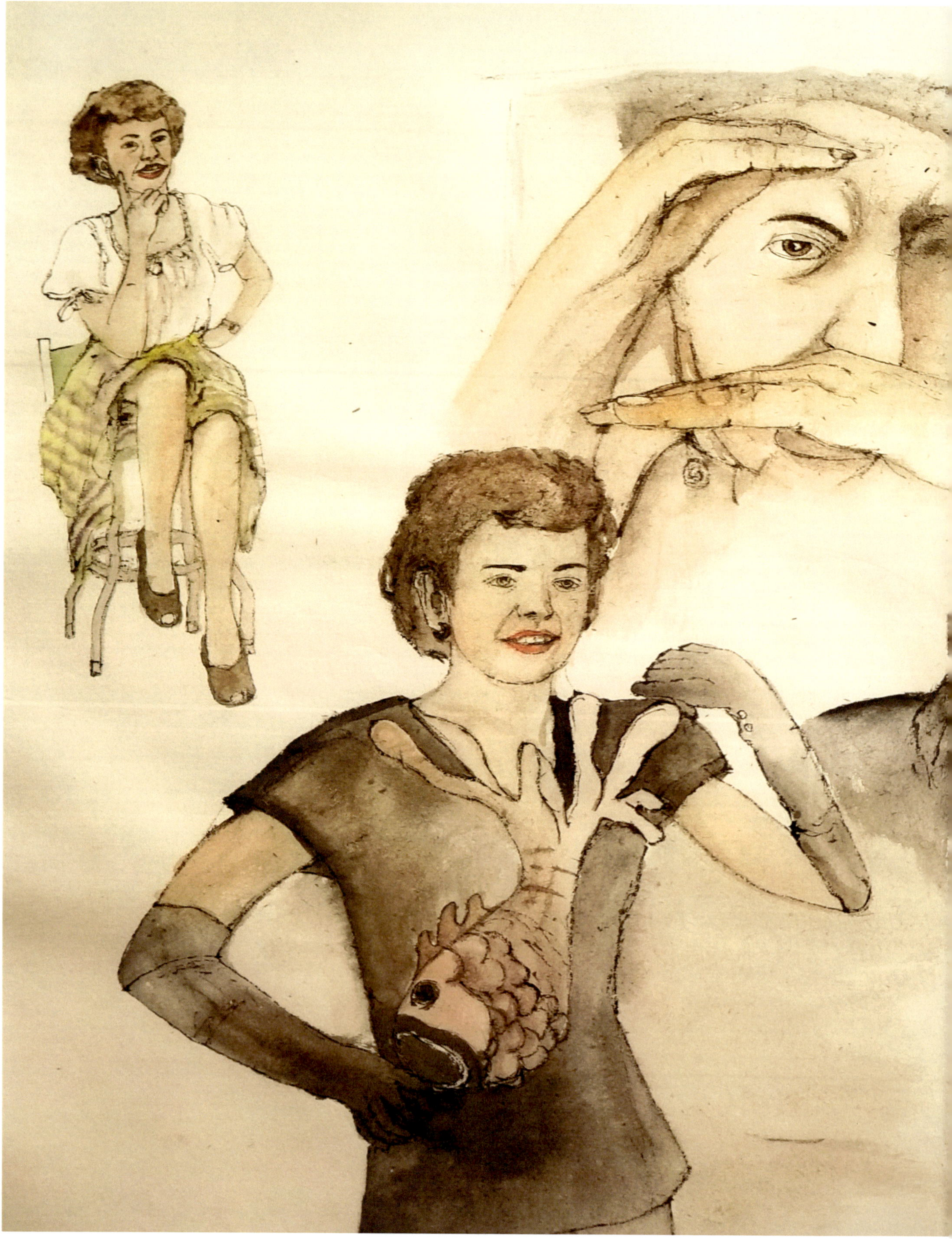

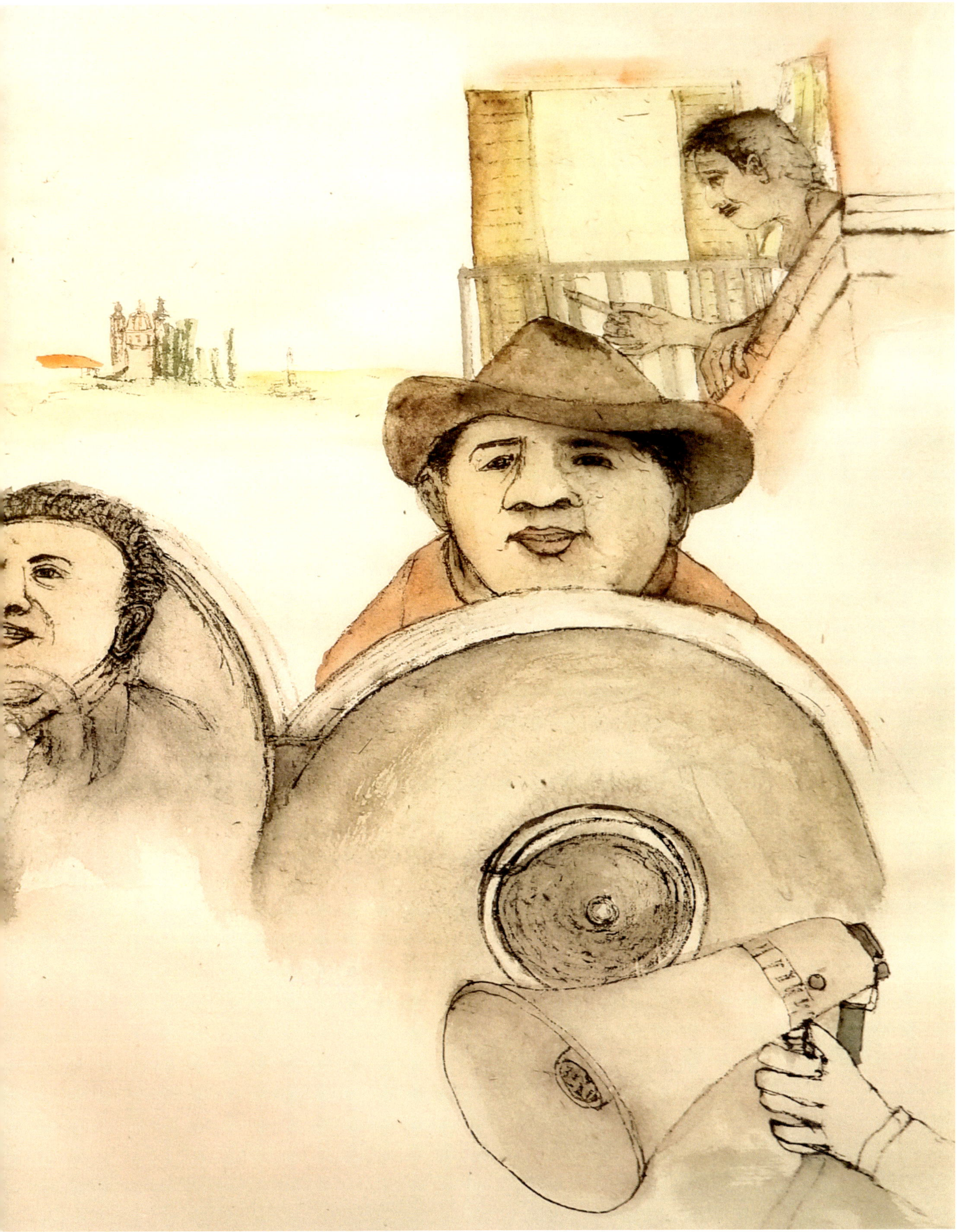

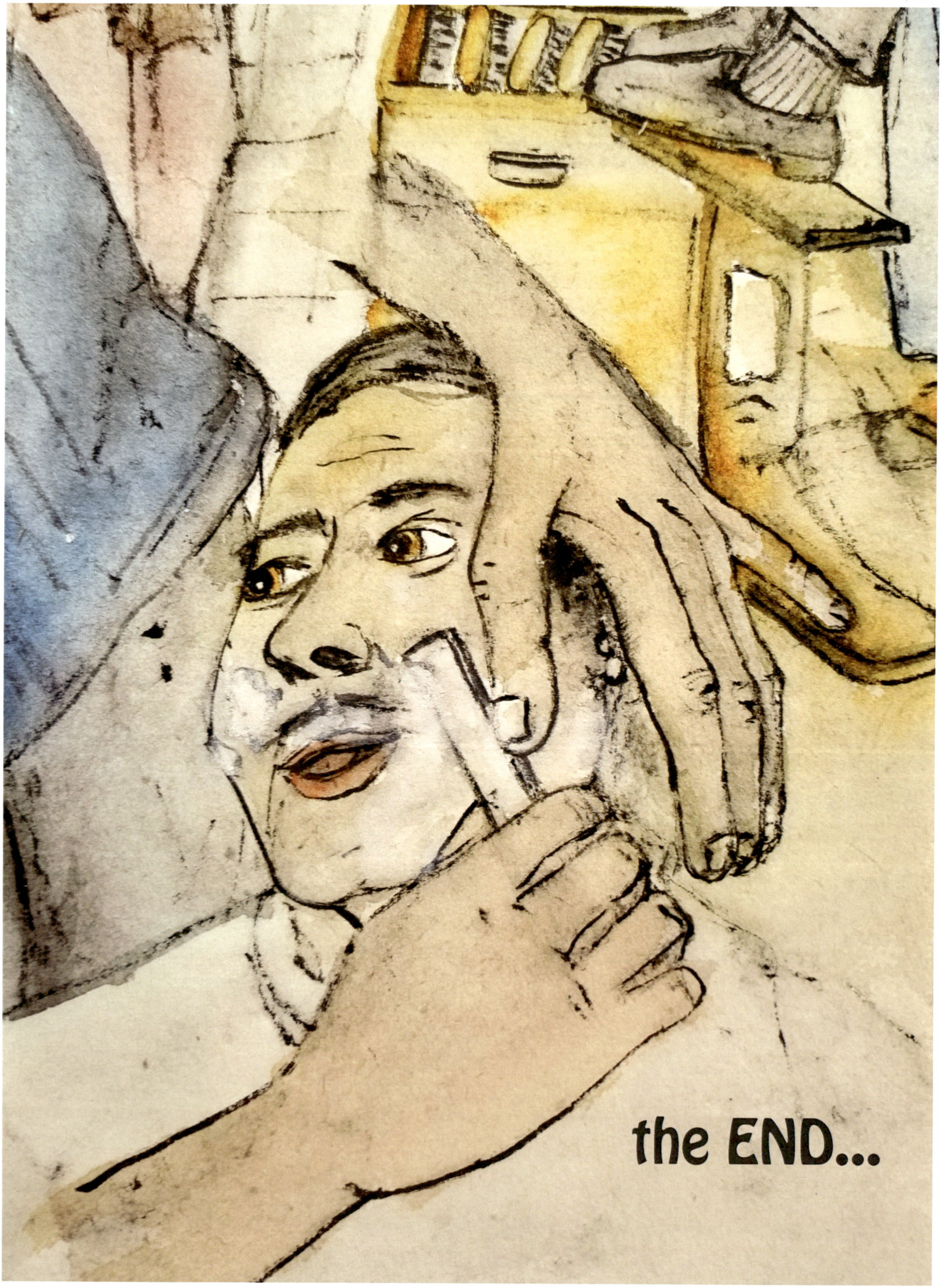
the END...

Lightning Source UK Ltd.
Milton Keynes UK
UKRC012043210119
335702UK00009B/30

9781389609831